Mediterranean Diet

Cookbook for Beginners UK

1600 Days of Simple, Balanced and Mouthwatering
Mediterranean Recipes with 28-Day Meal Plan to Boost
Immunity and Promote Heart Health

Lily Glover

CONTENTS

Introduction

Welcome to the world of Mediterranean cuisine! I am delighted to present to you my latest cookbook, "Mediterranean Diet Cookbook for Beginners UK." My name is Lily Glover, and I am a passionate chef and nutritionist with a deep love for the Mediterranean way of eating. This cookbook is a culmination of my personal journey and extensive research into the benefits of this wholesome and delicious diet.

Growing up in a Mediterranean household, I was fortunate to be exposed to the incredible flavors and health benefits of this cuisine from an early age. The Mediterranean diet is known for its emphasis on fresh fruits and vegetables, whole grains, lean proteins, and healthy fats, all of which contribute to its numerous health benefits.

As a nutritionist, I have witnessed the positive impact of the Mediterranean diet on individuals' overall well-being, particularly in terms of boosting immunity and promoting heart health. This realization motivated me to create a comprehensive cookbook that not only introduces the essence of Mediterranean cooking but also provides practical and easy-to-follow recipes for beginners.

"Mediterranean Diet Cookbook for Beginners UK" sets itself apart from other cookbooks by offering 1600 days' worth of recipes, ensuring a wide range of options for readers to enjoy. The cookbook is designed to cater to beginners, making it accessible to individuals who may be unfamiliar with the Mediterranean diet. The recipes are simple, balanced, and will appeal to both seasoned home cooks and those new to the kitchen.

A standout feature of this cookbook is the inclusion of a 28-day meal plan. This meal plan provides readers with a structured approach to adopting the Mediterranean diet, offering a clear roadmap for their culinary journey. The meal plan takes into account nutritional requirements, flavor diversity, and practicality, making it a valuable tool for readers seeking to make a positive change to their lifestyle.

Join me on an exciting Mediterranean journey as we explore the delights of nourishing and delicious meals that not only please our palates but also provide immense benefits to our overall health and well-being.

What is the Mediterranean Diet exactly?

The Mediterranean Diet is a dietary pattern inspired by the traditional eating habits of countries bordering the Mediterranean Sea. It is characterized by the consumption of plant-based foods, including fruits, vegetables, whole grains, legumes, and nuts, along with moderate amounts of fish, poultry, and dairy products. It also includes the use of healthy fats, such as olive oil, and encourages the moderate consumption of red wine.

What are the key principles of the Mediterranean Diet?

The key principles of the Mediterranean Diet include:

- **Emphasis on plant-based foods**

The Mediterranean Diet encourages the consumption of fruits, vegetables, whole grains, legumes, and nuts. These foods are rich in fiber, vitamins, minerals, and antioxidants.

- **Use of healthy fats**

The diet promotes the use of olive oil as the primary source of fat, which is high in monounsaturated fats and beneficial for heart health. Other sources of healthy fats include avocados, nuts, and seeds.

- **Moderate consumption of fish and poultry**

Fish, especially fatty fish like salmon, mackerel, and sardines, is a regular part of the Mediterranean Diet due to its high omega-3 fatty acid content. Poultry is also included but in moderate amounts.

- **Limited intake of red meat**

Red meat, such as beef and pork, is consumed in smaller quantities and less frequently in the Mediterranean Diet. Plant-based protein sources, like legumes and nuts, are often preferred.

- **Moderate consumption of dairy products**

Dairy products, such as yogurt and cheese, are included in moderation in the Mediterranean Diet. They provide calcium and protein but should be consumed in controlled portions.

- **Encouragement of whole grains**

Whole grains, such as whole wheat, oats, barley, and brown rice, are preferred over refined grains. These provide more fiber, vitamins, and minerals.

- **Consumption of fruits and vegetables**

The Mediterranean Diet promotes the intake of a variety of fruits and vegetables, which are nutrient-dense and contribute to overall health and well-being.

- **Use of herbs and spices**

Instead of relying on salt for flavoring, the Mediterranean Diet encourages the use of herbs and spices, such as basil, oregano, rosemary, garlic, and lemon, to enhance taste and reduce the need for excessive salt.

- **Enjoyment of meals with others**

The Mediterranean Diet emphasizes the social aspect of eating, such as sharing meals with family and friends. This promotes a positive relationship with food and encourages mindful eating.

- **Regular physical activity**

The Mediterranean Diet is not just about food choices but also incorporates regular physical activity. Engaging in activities such as walking, cycling, or gardening is an integral part of a healthy Mediterranean lifestyle.

The Mediterranean Diet is a flexible and adaptable approach, allowing for individual preferences and cultural variations. The key is to focus on whole, minimally processed foods, prioritize plant-based foods, and maintain a balanced and enjoyable eating pattern.

Is the Mediterranean Diet suitable for vegetarians or vegans?

Yes, the Mediterranean Diet can be suitable for vegetarians or vegans with some modifications. The traditional Mediterranean Diet is primarily plant-based and emphasizes fruits, vegetables, whole grains, legumes, nuts, and seeds. While it does include animal products such as fish, poultry, and dairy, these can be substituted or eliminated in a vegetarian or vegan version of the diet.

For vegetarians, dairy products and eggs can be included as sources of protein. Vegetarians following the Mediterranean Diet can incorporate yogurt, cheese, and eggs into their meals. They can also include plant-based proteins like legumes, tofu, tempeh, and seitan.

For vegans, dairy products and eggs are eliminated. However, they can still follow a plant-based version of the Mediterranean Diet by incorporating a variety of plant-based protein sources such as legumes, tofu, tempeh, seitan, and plant-based dairy alternatives like soy milk or almond milk. They can also focus on consuming a wide range of fruits, vegetables, whole grains, nuts, and seeds.

To ensure adequate nutrient intake, vegans following the Mediterranean Diet should pay attention to certain nutrients that may be lacking in a plant-based diet, such as vitamin B12, iron, and omega-3 fatty acids. They may need to consider fortified foods or supplements to meet their nutrient needs.

It's important for vegetarians and vegans to be mindful of their food choices and ensure they are getting a variety of nutrients from different plant-based sources.

What are the potential health benefits of following the Mediterranean Diet?

The Mediterranean Diet has been extensively studied and has been associated with numerous health benefits. Here are some potential health benefits of following the Mediterranean Diet:

- **Reduced risk of heart disease**

The Mediterranean Diet is known for its heart-healthy properties. It has been shown to reduce the risk of heart disease and lower levels of LDL (bad) cholesterol. The high intake of monounsaturated fats from olive oil, along with the consumption of fish rich in omega-3 fatty acids, may contribute to these benefits. Additionally, the diet is low in saturated fats and processed foods, which are known to increase the risk of heart disease.

- **Improved weight management**

The Mediterranean Diet is associated with better weight control and a lower risk of obesity. The emphasis on whole, minimally processed foods, including fruits, vegetables, whole grains, and lean protein sources, can contribute to a healthy weight. The high fiber content of the diet, combined with moderate portions and regular physical activity, may also help with weight management.

- **Lower risk of type 2 diabetes**

Following the Mediterranean Diet has been shown to reduce the risk of developing type 2 diabetes. The diet's emphasis on whole grains, legumes, fruits, vegetables, healthy fats, and lean protein sources may contribute to better blood sugar control and insulin sensitivity. Additionally, the diet's high fiber content can help regulate blood sugar levels.

- **Improved cognitive function**

The Mediterranean Diet has been associated with a reduced risk of cognitive decline and improved cognitive function, particularly in older adults. The high intake of antioxidant-rich fruits and vegetables, along with the consumption of healthy fats and omega-3 fatty acids, may have neuroprotective effects and help maintain brain health.

- **Improved gut health**

The Mediterranean Diet, with its emphasis on whole foods and high fiber content, can promote a healthy gut microbiome. The consumption of fruits, vegetables, legumes, and whole grains provides prebiotic fibers that support the growth of beneficial gut bacteria. A healthy gut microbiome is associated with various health benefits, including improved digestion, immune function, and mental health.

- **Reduced inflammation**

Chronic inflammation is a key driver of many chronic diseases. The Mediterranean Diet, with its emphasis on anti-inflammatory foods, can help reduce inflammation in the body. Olive oil, fatty fish, nuts, fruits, vegetables, and herbs and spices, commonly consumed in the Mediterranean Diet, have anti-inflammatory properties that may help protect against chronic diseases.

- **Improved overall longevity**

Following the Mediterranean Diet has been associated with a longer lifespan and reduced mortality rates. The combination of the diet's nutrient-dense foods, healthy fats, plant-based focus, and moderate alcohol consumption may contribute to overall health and well-being.

The Mediterranean Diet is not a cure-all or a guarantee of good health. Other lifestyle factors, such as regular physical activity, adequate sleep, and stress management, also play a significant role in overall health.

Breakfast Recipes

Napoli Scrambled Eggs With Anchovies

Servings:4
Cooking Time:20 Minutes
Ingredients:
- 2 tbsp olive oil
- 1 green bell pepper, chopped
- 2 anchovy fillets, chopped
- 8 cherry tomatoes, cubed
- 2 spring onions, chopped
- 1 tbsp capers, drained
- 5 black olives, pitted and sliced
- 6 eggs, beaten
- Salt and black pepper to taste
- ¼ tsp dried oregano
- 1 tbsp parsley, chopped

Directions:
1. Warm the olive oil in a skillet over medium heat and cook the bell pepper and spring onions for 3 minutes. Add in anchovies, cherry tomatoes, capers, and black olives and cook for another 2 minutes. Stir in eggs and sprinkle with salt, pepper, and oregano and scramble for 5 minutes. Serve sprinkled with parsley.

Nutrition Info:
- Info Per Serving: Calories: 260;Fat: 18g;Protein: 12g;Carbs: 12g.

Fresh Mozzarella & Salmon Frittata

Servings:4
Cooking Time:15 Minutes
Ingredients:
- 1 ball fresh mozzarella cheese, chopped
- 2 tsp olive oil
- 8 fresh eggs
- ½ cup whole milk
- 1 spring onion, chopped
- ¼ cup chopped fresh basil
- Salt and black pepper to taste
- 3 oz smoked salmon, chopped

Directions:
1. Preheat your broiler to medium. Whisk the eggs with milk, spring onion, basil, pepper, and salt in a bowl. Heat the olive oil in a skillet over medium heat and pour in the egg mixture.
2. Top with mozzarella cheese and cook for 3–5 minutes until the frittata is set on the bottom and the egg is almost set but still moist on top. Scatter over the salmon and place the skillet under the preheated broiler for 1-2 minutes or until set and slightly puffed. Cut the frittata into wedges. Enjoy!

Nutrition Info:
- Info Per Serving: Calories: 351;Fat: 13g;Protein: 52g;Carbs: 6g.

Open-faced Margherita Sandwiches

Servings:4
Cooking Time: 5 Minutes
Ingredients:
- 2 whole-wheat submarine or hoagie rolls, sliced open horizontally
- 1 tablespoon extra-virgin olive oil
- 1 garlic clove, halved
- 1 large ripe tomato, cut into 8 slices
- ¼ teaspoon dried oregano
- 1 cup fresh Mozzarella, sliced
- ¼ cup lightly packed fresh basil leaves, torn into small pieces
- ¼ teaspoon freshly ground black pepper

Directions:
1. Preheat the broiler to High with the rack 4 inches under the heating element.
2. Put the sliced bread on a large, rimmed baking sheet and broil for 1 minute, or until the bread is just lightly toasted. Remove from the oven.
3. Brush each piece of the toasted bread with the oil, and rub a garlic half over each piece.
4. Put the toasted bread back on the baking sheet. Evenly divide the tomato slices on each piece. Sprinkle with the oregano and top with the cheese.
5. Place the baking sheet under the broiler. Set the timer for 1½ minutes, but check after 1 minute. When the cheese is melted and the edges are just starting to get dark brown, remove the sandwiches from the oven.
6. Top each sandwich with the fresh basil and pepper before serving.

Nutrition Info:
- Info Per Serving: Calories: 93;Fat: 2.0g;Protein: 10.0g;Carbs: 8.0g.

Apple & Date Smoothie

Servings:1
Cooking Time:5 Minutes
Ingredients:
- 1 apple, peeled and chopped
- ½ cup milk
- 4 dates
- 1 tsp ground cinnamon

Directions:
1. In a blender, place the milk, ½ cup of water, dates, cinnamon, and apple. Blitz until smooth. Let chill in the fridge for 30 minutes. Serve in a tall glass.

Nutrition Info:
- Info Per Serving: Calories: 486;Fat: 29g;Protein: 4.2g;Carbs: 63g.

White Pizzas With Arugula And Spinach

Servings:4
Cooking Time: 20 Minutes
Ingredients:

- 1 pound refrigerated fresh pizza dough
- 2 tablespoons extra-virgin olive oil, divided
- ½ cup thinly sliced onion
- 2 garlic cloves, minced
- 3 cups baby spinach
- 3 cups arugula
- 1 tablespoon water
- ¼ teaspoon freshly ground black pepper
- 1 tablespoon freshly squeezed lemon juice
- ½ cup shredded Parmesan cheese
- ½ cup crumbled goat cheese
- Cooking spray

Directions:

1. Preheat the oven to 500ºF. Spritz a large, rimmed baking sheet with cooking spray.
2. Take the pizza dough out of the refrigerator.
3. Heat 1 tablespoon of the oil in a large skillet over medium heat. Add the onion to the skillet and cook for 4 minutes, stirring constantly. Add the garlic and cook for 1 minute, stirring constantly.
4. Stir in the spinach, arugula, water and pepper. Cook for about 2 minutes, stirring constantly, or until all the greens are coated with oil and they start to cook down. Remove the skillet from the heat and drizzle with the lemon juice.
5. On a lightly floured work surface, form the pizza dough into a 12-inch circle or a 10-by-12-inch rectangle, using a rolling pin or by stretching with your hands.
6. Place the dough on the prepared baking sheet. Brush the dough with the remaining 1 tablespoon of the oil. Spread the cooked greens on top of the dough to within ½ inch of the edge. Top with the Parmesan cheese and goat cheese.
7. Bake in the preheated oven for 10 to 12 minutes, or until the crust starts to brown around the edges.
8. Remove from the oven and transfer the pizza to a cutting board. Cut into eight pieces before serving.

Nutrition Info:

- Info Per Serving: Calories: 521;Fat: 31.0g;Protein: 23.0g;Carbs: 38.0g.

Brown Rice Salad With Cheese

Servings:4
Cooking Time:10 Minutes
Ingredients:

- 2 tbsp olive oil
- ½ cup brown rice
- 1 lb watercress
- 1 Roma tomato, sliced
- 4 oz feta cheese, crumbled
- 2 tbsp fresh basil, chopped
- Salt and black pepper to taste
- 2 tbsp lemon juice
- ¼ tsp lemon zest

Directions:

1. Bring to a boil salted water in a pot over medium heat. Add in the rice and cook for 15-18 minutes. Drain and let cool completely. Whisk the olive oil, lemon zest, lemon juice, salt, and pepper in a salad bowl. Add in the watercress, cooled rice, and basil and toss to coat. Top with feta cheese and tomato. Serve immediately.

Nutrition Info:

- Info Per Serving: Calories: 480;Fat: 24g;Protein: 14g;Carbs: 55g.

Dulse, Avocado, And Tomato Pitas

Servings:4
Cooking Time: 30 Minutes
Ingredients:

- 2 teaspoons coconut oil
- ½ cup dulse, picked through and separated
- Ground black pepper, to taste
- 2 avocados, sliced
- 2 tablespoons lime juice
- ¼ cup chopped cilantro
- 2 scallions, white and light green parts, sliced
- Sea salt, to taste
- 4 whole wheat pitas, sliced in half
- 4 cups chopped romaine
- 4 plum tomatoes, sliced

Directions:

1. Heat the coconut oil in a nonstick skillet over medium heat until melted.
2. Add the dulse and sauté for 5 minutes or until crispy. Sprinkle with ground black pepper and turn off the heat. Set aside.
3. Put the avocado, lime juice, cilantro, and scallions in a food processor and sprinkle with salt and ground black pepper. Pulse to combine well until smooth.
4. Toast the pitas in a baking pan in the oven for 1 minute until soft.
5. Transfer the pitas to a clean work surface and open. Spread the avocado mixture over the pitas, then top with dulse, romaine, and tomato slices.
6. Serve immediately.

Nutrition Info:

- Info Per Serving: Calories: 412;Fat: 18.7g;Protein: 9.1g;Carbs: 56.1g.

Anchovy & Spinach Sandwiches

Servings:2
Cooking Time:5 Minutes
Ingredients:

- 1 avocado, mashed
- 4 anchovies, drained
- 4 whole-wheat bread slices
- 1 cup baby spinach
- 1 tomato, sliced

Directions:

1. Spread the slices of bread with avocado mash and arrange the anchovies over. Top with baby spinach and tomato slices.

Nutrition Info:

- Info Per Serving: Calories: 300;Fat: 12g;Protein: 5g;Carbs: 10g.

Falafel Balls With Tahini Sauce

Servings:4
Cooking Time: 20 Minutes
Ingredients:

- Tahini Sauce:
- ½ cup tahini
- 2 tablespoons lemon juice
- ¼ cup finely chopped flat-leaf parsley
- 2 cloves garlic, minced
- ½ cup cold water, as needed
- Falafel:
- 1 cup dried chickpeas, soaked overnight, drained
- ¼ cup chopped flat-leaf parsley
- ¼ cup chopped cilantro
- 1 large onion, chopped
- 1 teaspoon cumin
- ½ teaspoon chili flakes
- 4 cloves garlic
- 1 teaspoon sea salt
- 5 tablespoons almond flour
- 1½ teaspoons baking soda, dissolved in 1 teaspoon water
- 2 cups peanut oil
- 1 medium bell pepper, chopped
- 1 medium tomato, chopped
- 4 whole-wheat pita breads

Directions:

1. Make the Tahini Sauce:
2. Combine the ingredients for the tahini sauce in a small bowl. Stir to mix well until smooth.
3. Wrap the bowl in plastic and refrigerate until ready to serve.
4. Make the Falafel:
5. Put the chickpeas, parsley, cilantro, onion, cumin, chili flakes, garlic, and salt in a food processor. Pulse to mix well but not puréed.
6. Add the flour and baking soda to the food processor, then pulse to form a smooth and tight dough.
7. Put the dough in a large bowl and wrap in plastic. Refrigerate for at least 2 hours to let it rise.
8. Divide and shape the dough into walnut-sized small balls.
9. Pour the peanut oil in a large pot and heat over high heat until the temperature of the oil reaches 375°F.
10. Drop 6 balls into the oil each time, and fry for 5 minutes or until golden brown and crispy. Turn the balls with a strainer to make them fried evenly.
11. Transfer the balls on paper towels with the strainer, then drain the oil from the balls.
12. Roast the pita breads in the oven for 5 minutes or until golden brown, if needed, then stuff the pitas with falafel balls and top with bell peppers and tomatoes. Drizzle with tahini sauce and serve immediately.

Nutrition Info:

- Info Per Serving: Calories: 574;Fat: 27.1g;Protein: 19.8g;Carbs: 69.7g.

Baked Ricotta With Honey Pears

Servings:4
Cooking Time: 22 To 25 Minutes
Ingredients:

- 1 container whole-milk ricotta cheese
- 2 large eggs
- ¼ cup whole-wheat pastry flour
- 1 tablespoon sugar
- 1 teaspoon vanilla extract
- ¼ teaspoon ground nutmeg
- 1 pear, cored and diced
- 2 tablespoons water
- 1 tablespoon honey
- Nonstick cooking spray

Directions:

1. Preheat the oven to 400°F. Spray four ramekins with nonstick cooking spray.
2. Beat together the ricotta, eggs, flour, sugar, vanilla, and nutmeg in a large bowl until combined. Spoon the mixture into the ramekins.
3. Bake in the preheated oven for 22 to 25 minutes, or until the ricotta is just set.
4. Meanwhile, in a small saucepan over medium heat, simmer the pear in the water for 10 minutes, or until slightly softened. Remove from the heat, and stir in the honey.
5. Remove the ramekins from the oven and cool slightly on a wire rack. Top the ricotta ramekins with the pear and serve.

Nutrition Info:

- Info Per Serving: Calories: 329;Fat: 19.0g;Protein: 17.0g;Carbs: 23.0g.

Honey & Feta Frozen Yogurt

Servings:4
Cooking Time:5 Minutes + Freezing Time
Ingredients:

- 1 tbsp honey
- 1 cup Greek yogurt
- ½ cup feta cheese, crumbled
- 2 tbsp mint leaves, chopped

Directions:
1. In a food processor, blend yogurt, honey, and feta cheese until smooth. Transfer to a wide dish, cover with plastic wrap, and put in the freezer for 2 hours or until solid. When frozen, spoon into cups, sprinkle with mint, and serve.

Nutrition Info:

- Info Per Serving: Calories: 170;Fat: 12g;Protein: 7g;Carbs: 13g.

Samosas In Potatoes

Servings:8
Cooking Time: 30 Minutes
Ingredients:

- 4 small potatoes
- 1 teaspoon coconut oil
- 1 small onion, finely chopped
- 1 small piece ginger, minced
- 2 garlic cloves, minced
- 2 to 3 teaspoons curry powder
- Sea salt and freshly ground black pepper, to taste
- ¼ cup frozen peas, thawed
- 2 carrots, grated
- ¼ cup chopped fresh cilantro

Directions:
1. Preheat the oven to 350ºF.
2. Poke small holes into potatoes with a fork, then wrap with aluminum foil.
3. Bake in the preheated oven for 30 minutes until tender.
4. Meanwhile, heat the coconut oil in a nonstick skillet over medium-high heat until melted.
5. Add the onion and sauté for 5 minutes or until translucent.
6. Add the ginger and garlic to the skillet and sauté for 3 minutes or until fragrant.
7. Add the curry power, salt, and ground black pepper, then stir to coat the onion. Remove them from the heat.
8. When the cooking of potatoes is complete, remove the potatoes from the foil and slice in half.
9. Hollow to potato halves with a spoon, then combine the potato fresh with sautéed onion, peas, carrots, and cilantro in a large bowl. Stir to mix well.
10. Spoon the mixture back to the tomato skins and serve immediately.

Nutrition Info:

- Info Per Serving: Calories: 131;Fat: 13.9g;Protein: 3.2g;Carbs: 8.8g.

Luxurious Fruit Cocktail

Servings:6
Cooking Time:10 Min + Cooling Time
Ingredients:

- ½ cup olive oil
- 2 cups cubed honeydew melon
- 2 cups cubed cantaloupe
- 2 cups red seedless grapes
- 1 lemon, juiced and zested
- ½ cup slivered almonds
- 1 cup sliced strawberries
- 1 cup blueberries
- ¼ cup honey

Directions:
1. In a bowl, place melon, cantaloupe, grapes, strawberries, blueberries, and lemon zest. Toss to coat and set aside.
2. Mix the honey and lemon juice in a bowl and whisk until the honey is well incorporated. Carefully pour in the olive oil and mix well. Drizzle over the fruit and toss to combine. Transfer to the fridge covered and let chill for at least 4 hours. Stir well and top with slivered almonds before serving.

Nutrition Info:

- Info Per Serving: Calories: 326;Fat: 19g;Protein: 2g;Carbs: 43g.

Tomato Eggs With Fried Potatoes

Servings:2
Cooking Time:20 Minutes
Ingredients:

- 2 tbsp + ½ cup olive oil
- 3 medium tomatoes, puréed
- 1 tbsp fresh tarragon, chopped
- 1 garlic clove, minced
- Salt and black pepper to taste
- 3 potatoes, cubed
- 4 fresh eggs
- 1 tsp fresh oregano, chopped

Directions:

1. Warm 2 tbsp of olive oil in a saucepan over medium heat. Add the garlic and sauté for 1 minute. Pour in the tomatoes, tarragon, salt, and pepper. Reduce the heat and cook for 5-8 minutes or until the sauce is thickened and bubbly.
2. Warm the remaining olive oil in a skillet over medium heat. Fry the potatoes for 5 minutes until crisp and browned on the outside, then cover and reduce heat to low. Steam potatoes until done. Carefully crack the eggs into the tomato sauce.
3. Cook over low heat until the eggs are set in the sauce, about 6 minutes. Remove the potatoes from the pan, drain them on paper towels, and place them in a bowl. Sprinkle with salt and pepper and top with oregano. Carefully remove the eggs with a slotted spoon and place them on a plate with the potatoes. Spoon sauce over and serve.

Nutrition Info:

- Info Per Serving: Calories: 1146;Fat: 69g;Protein: 26g;Carbs: 45g.

Turkish Eggplant And Tomatoes Pide With Mint

Servings:6
Cooking Time: 20 Minutes
Ingredients:

- Dough:
- 3 cups almond flour
- 2 teaspoons raw honey
- ½ teaspoon instant or rapid-rise yeast
- 1⅓ cups ice water
- 1 tablespoon extra-virgin olive oil
- 1½ teaspoons sea salt
- Eggplant and Tomato Toppings:
- 28 ounces whole tomatoes, peeled and puréed
- 5 tablespoons extra-virgin olive oil, divided
- 1 pound eggplant, cut into ½-inch pieces
- ½ red bell pepper, chopped
- Sea salt and ground black pepper, to taste
- 3 garlic cloves, minced
- ¼ teaspoon red pepper flakes
- ½ teaspoon smoked paprika
- 6 tablespoons minced fresh mint, divided
- 1½ cups crumbled feta cheese

Directions:

1. Make the Dough:
2. Combine the flour, yeast, and honey in a food processor, pulse to combine well. Gently add water while pulsing. Let the dough sit for 10 minutes.
3. Mix the olive oil and salt in the dough and knead the dough until smooth. Wrap in plastic and refrigerate for at least 1 day.
4. Make the Toppings:
5. Heat 2 tablespoons of olive oil in a nonstick skillet over medium-high heat until shimmering.
6. Add the bell pepper, eggplant, and ½ teaspoon of salt. Sauté for 6 minutes or until the eggplant is lightly browned.
7. Add the red pepper flakes, paprika, and garlic. Sauté for 1 minute or until fragrant.
8. Pour in the puréed tomatoes. Bring to a simmer, then cook for 10 minutes or until the mixture is thickened into about 3½ cups.
9. Turn off the heat and mix in 4 tablespoons of mint, salt, and ground black pepper. Set them aside until ready to use.
10. Make the Turkish Pide:
11. Preheat the oven to 500ºF. Line three baking sheets with parchment papers.
12. On a clean work surface, divide and shape the dough into six 14 by 5-inch ovals. Transfer the dough to the baking sheets.
13. Brush them with 3 tablespoons of olive oil and spread the eggplant mixture and feta cheese on top.
14. Bake in the preheated oven for 12 minutes or until golden brown. Rotate the pide halfway through the baking time.
15. Remove the pide from the oven and spread with remaining mint and serve immediately.

Nutrition Info:

- Info Per Serving: Calories: 500;Fat: 22.1g;Protein: 8.0g;Carbs: 69.7g.

Couscous & Cucumber Bowl

Servings:4
Cooking Time:15 Minutes
Ingredients:

- 2 tbsp olive oil
- ¾ cup couscous
- 1 cup water
- 1 yellow onion, chopped
- 2 garlic cloves, minced
- 2 cups canned chickpeas
- Salt to taste
- 15 oz canned tomatoes, diced
- 1 cucumber, cut into ribbons
- ½ cup black olives, chopped
- 1 tbsp lemon juice
- 1 tbsp mint leaves, chopped

Directions:

1. Cover the couscous with salted boiling water, cover, and let it sit for about 5 minutes. Then fluff with a fork and set aside.
2. Warm the olive oil in a skillet over medium heat and sauté onion and garlic for 3 minutes until soft. Stir in chickpeas, salt, and tomatoes for 1-2 minutes. Turn off the heat and mix in olives, couscous, and lemon juice. Transfer to a bowl and top with cucumber ribbons and mint to serve.

Nutrition Info:

- Info Per Serving: Calories: 350;Fat: 11g;Protein: 12g;Carbs: 50g.

Artichoke & Spinach Frittata

Servings:4
Cooking Time:55 Minutes
Ingredients:

- 4 oz canned artichokes, chopped
- 2 tsp olive oil
- ½ cup whole milk
- 8 eggs
- 1 cup spinach, chopped
- 1 garlic clove, minced
- ½ cup Parmesan, crumbled
- 1 tsp oregano, dried
- 1 Jalapeño pepper, minced
- Salt to taste

Directions:

1. Preheat oven to 360 F. Warm the olive oil in a skillet over medium heat and sauté garlic and spinach for 3 minutes.
2. Beat the eggs in a bowl. Stir in artichokes, milk, Parmesan cheese, oregano, jalapeño pepper, and salt. Add in spinach mixture and toss to combine. Transfer to a greased baking dish and bake for 20 minutes until golden and bubbling. Slice into wedges and serve.

Nutrition Info:

- Info Per Serving: Calories: 190;Fat: 14g;Protein: 10g;Carbs: 5g.

Mozzarella & Olive Cakes

Servings:6
Cooking Time:25 Minutes
Ingredients:

- 4 tbsp olive oil, softened
- ¼ cup mozzarella, shredded
- ¼ cup black olives, chopped
- ½ cup milk
- 1 egg, beaten
- 1 cup cornflour
- 1 tsp baking powder
- 3 sun-dried tomatoes, chopped
- 2 tbsp fresh cilantro, chopped
- ¼ tsp kosher salt

Directions:

1. Preheat oven to 360 °F. In a bowl, whisk the egg with milk and olive oil. In a separate bowl, mix the salt, cornflour, cilantro, and baking powder. Combine the wet ingredients with the dry mixture. Stir in black olives, tomatoes, and mozzarella cheese. Pour the mixture into greased ramekins and bake for 18-20 minutes or until cooked and golden.

Nutrition Info:

- Info Per Serving: Calories: 189;Fat: 11.7g;Protein: 4g;Carbs: 19g.

Veg Mix And Blackeye Pea Burritos

Servings:6
Cooking Time: 40 Minutes
Ingredients:
- 1 teaspoon olive oil
- 1 red onion, diced
- 2 garlic cloves, minced
- 1 zucchini, chopped
- 1 tomato, diced
- 1 bell pepper, any color, deseeded and diced
- 1 can blackeye peas
- 2 teaspoons chili powder
- Sea salt, to taste
- 6 whole-grain tortillas

Directions:
1. Preheat the oven to 325°F.
2. Heat the olive oil in a nonstick skillet over medium heat or until shimmering.
3. Add the onion and sauté for 5 minutes or until translucent.
4. Add the garlic and sauté for 30 seconds or until fragrant.
5. Add the zucchini and sauté for 5 minutes or until tender.
6. Add the tomato and bell pepper and sauté for 2 minutes or until soft.
7. Fold in the black peas and sprinkle them with chili powder and salt. Stir to mix well.
8. Place the tortillas on a clean work surface, then top them with sautéed vegetables mix.
9. Fold one ends of tortillas over the vegetable mix, then tuck and roll them into burritos.
10. Arrange the burritos in a baking dish, seam side down, then pour the juice remains in the skillet over the burritos.
11. Bake in the preheated oven for 25 minutes or until golden brown.
12. Serve immediately.

Nutrition Info:
- Info Per Serving: Calories: 335;Fat: 16.2g;Protein: 12.1g;Carbs: 8.3g.

Fluffy Almond Flour Pancakes With Strawberries

Servings:4
Cooking Time: 15 Minutes
Ingredients:
- 1 cup plus 2 tablespoons unsweetened almond milk
- 1 cup almond flour
- 2 large eggs, whisked
- ⅓ cup honey
- 1 teaspoon baking soda
- ¼ teaspoon salt
- 2 tablespoons extra-virgin olive oil
- 1 cup sliced strawberries

Directions:
1. Combine the almond milk, almond flour, whisked eggs, honey, baking soda, and salt in a large bowl and whisk to incorporate.
2. Heat the olive oil in a large skillet over medium-high heat.
3. Make the pancakes: Pour ⅓ cup of batter into the hot skillet and swirl the pan so the batter covers the bottom evenly. Cook for 2 to 3 minutes until the pancake turns golden brown around the edges. Gently flip the pancake with a spatula and cook for 2 to 3 minutes until cooked through. Repeat with the remaining batter.
4. Serve the pancakes with the sliced strawberries on top.

Nutrition Info:
- Info Per Serving: Calories: 298;Fat: 11.7g;Protein: 11.8g;Carbs: 34.8g.

Vegetable Polenta With Fried Eggs

Servings:4
Cooking Time:35 Minutes
Ingredients:

- 2 tbsp butter
- ½ tsp sea salt
- 1 cup polenta
- 4 eggs
- 2 spring onions, chopped
- 1 bell pepper, chopped
- 1 zucchini, chopped
- 1 tsp ginger-garlic paste
- 1 ½ cups vegetable broth
- ¼ tsp chili flakes, crushed
- 2 tbsp basil leaves, chopped

Directions:

1. Melt 1 tbsp of the butter in a skillet over medium heat. Place in spring onions, ginger-garlic paste, bell pepper, and zucchini and sauté for 5 minutes; set aside.
2. Pour the broth and 1 ½ cups of water in a pot and bring to a boil. Gradually whisk in polenta to avoid chunks, lower the heat, and simmer for 4-5 minutes. Keep whisking until it begins to thicken. Cook covered for 20 minutes, stirring often. Add the zucchini mixture, chili flakes, and salt and stir.
3. Heat the remaining butter in a skillet. Break the eggs and fry them until set and well cooked. Divide the polenta between bowls, top with fried eggs and basil, and serve.

Nutrition Info:

- Info Per Serving: Calories: 295;Fat: 12g;Protein: 11g;Carbs: 36g.

Spicy Black Bean And Poblano Dippers

Servings:8
Cooking Time: 21 Minutes
Ingredients:

- 2 tablespoons avocado oil, plus more for brushing the dippers
- 1 can black beans, drained and rinsed
- 1 poblano, deseeded and quartered
- 1 jalapeño, halved and deseeded
- ½ cup fresh cilantro, leaves and tender stems
- 1 yellow onion, quartered
- 2 garlic cloves
- 1 teaspoon chili powder
- 1 teaspoon ground cumin
- 1 teaspoon sea salt
- 24 organic corn tortillas

Directions:

1. Preheat the oven to 400ºF. Line a baking sheet with parchment paper and grease with avocado oil.
2. Combine the remaining ingredients, except for the tortillas, in a food processor, then pulse until chopped finely and the mixture holds together. Make sure not to purée the mixture.
3. Warm the tortillas on the baking sheet in the preheated oven for 1 minute or until softened.
4. Add a tablespoon of the mixture in the middle of each tortilla. Fold one side of the tortillas over the mixture and tuck to roll them up tightly to make the dippers.
5. Arrange the dippers on the baking sheet and brush them with avocado oil. Bake in the oven for 20 minutes or until well browned. Flip the dippers halfway through the cooking time.
6. Serve immediately.

Nutrition Info:

- Info Per Serving: Calories: 388;Fat: 6.5g;Protein: 16.2g;Carbs: 69.6g.

Berry-yogurt Smoothie

Servings:1
Cooking Time:5 Minutes
Ingredients:
- ½ cup Greek yogurt
- ¼ cup milk
- ½ cup fresh blueberries
- 1 tsp vanilla sugar
- 2 ice cubes

Directions:
1. Pulse the Greek yogurt, milk, vanilla sugar, and berries in your blender until the berries are liquefied. Add the ice cubes and blend on high until thick and smooth. Serve.

Nutrition Info:
- Info Per Serving: Calories: 230;Fat: 8.8g;Protein: 16g;Carbs: 23g.

Honey Breakfast Smoothie

Servings:1
Cooking Time:10 Minutes
Ingredients:
- 1 tbsp olive oil
- 2 tbsp almond butter
- 1 cup almond milk
- ¼ cup blueberries
- 1 tbsp ground flaxseed
- 1 tsp honey
- ½ tsp vanilla extract
- ¼ tsp ground cinnamon

Directions:
1. In a blender, mix the almond milk, blueberries, almond butter, flaxseed, olive oil, stevia vanilla, and cinnamon and pulse until smooth and creamy. Add more milk or water to achieve your desired consistency. Serve at room temperature.

Nutrition Info:
- Info Per Serving: Calories: 460;Fat: 40.2g;Protein: 9g;Carbs: 20g.

Granola & Berry Parfait

Servings:2
Cooking Time:5 Minutes
Ingredients:
- 2 cups berries
- 1 ½ cups Greek yogurt
- 1 tbsp powdered sugar
- ¼ cup granola

Directions:
1. Divide between two bowls a layer of berries, yogurt, and powdered sugar. Scatter with granola and serve.

Nutrition Info:
- Info Per Serving: Calories: 244;Fat: 11g;Protein: 21g;Carbs: 43g.

Fish And Seafood Recipes

Italian Tilapia Pilaf

Servings:2
Cooking Time:45 Minutes
Ingredients:
- 3 tbsp olive oil
- 2 tilapia fillets, boneless
- ½ tsp Italian seasoning
- ½ cup brown rice
- ½ cup green bell pepper, diced
- ½ cup white onions, chopped
- ½ tsp garlic powder
- Salt and black pepper to taste

Directions:
1. Warm 1 tbsp of olive oil in a saucepan over medium heat. Cook onions, bell pepper, garlic powder, Italian seasoning, salt, and pepper for 3 minutes. Stir in brown rice and 2 cups of water and bring to a simmer. Cook for 18 minutes. Warm the remaining oil in a skillet over medium heat. Season the tilapia with salt and pepper. Fry for 10 minutes on both sides. Share the rice among plates and top with the tilapia fillets.

Nutrition Info:
- Info Per Serving: Calories: 270;Fat: 18g;Protein: 13g;Carbs: 26g.

Spicy Haddock Stew

Servings:6
Cooking Time: 35 Minutes
Ingredients:
- ¼ cup coconut oil
- 1 tablespoon minced garlic
- 1 onion, chopped
- 2 celery stalks, chopped
- ½ fennel bulb, thinly sliced
- 1 carrot, diced
- 1 sweet potato, diced
- 1 can low-sodium diced tomatoes
- 1 cup coconut milk
- 1 cup low-sodium chicken broth
- ¼ teaspoon red pepper flakes
- 12 ounces haddock, cut into 1-inch chunks
- 2 tablespoons chopped fresh cilantro, for garnish

Directions:
1. In a large saucepan, heat the coconut oil over medium-high heat.
2. Add the garlic, onion, and celery and sauté for about 4 minutes, stirring occasionally, or until they are tender.
3. Stir in the fennel bulb, carrot, and sweet potato and sauté for 4 minutes more.
4. Add the diced tomatoes, coconut milk, chicken broth, and red pepper flakes and stir to incorporate, then bring the mixture to a boil.
5. Once it starts to boil, reduce the heat to low, and bring to a simmer for about 15 minutes, or until the vegetables are fork-tender.
6. Add the haddock chunks and continue simmering for about 10 minutes, or until the fish is cooked through.
7. Sprinkle the cilantro on top for garnish before serving.

Nutrition Info:
- Info Per Serving: Calories: 276;Fat: 20.9g;Protein: 14.2g;Carbs: 6.8g.

Salt And Pepper Calamari And Scallops

Servings:4
Cooking Time: 10 Minutes
Ingredients:

- 8 ounces calamari steaks, cut into ½-inch-thick rings
- 8 ounces sea scallops
- 1½ teaspoons salt, divided
- 1 teaspoon garlic powder
- 1 teaspoon freshly ground black pepper
- ⅓ cup extra-virgin olive oil
- 2 tablespoons almond butter

Directions:

1. Place the calamari and scallops on several layers of paper towels and pat dry. Sprinkle with 1 teaspoon of salt and allow to sit for 15 minutes at room temperature. Pat dry with additional paper towels. Sprinkle with pepper and garlic powder.
2. In a deep medium skillet, heat the olive oil and butter over medium-high heat. When the oil is hot but not smoking, add the scallops and calamari in a single layer to the skillet and sprinkle with the remaining ½ teaspoon of salt. Cook for 2 to 4 minutes on each side, depending on the size of the scallops, until just golden but still slightly opaque in center.
3. Using a slotted spoon, remove from the skillet and transfer to a serving platter. Allow the cooking oil to cool slightly and drizzle over the seafood before serving.

Nutrition Info:

- Info Per Serving: Calories: 309;Fat: 25.0g;Protein: 18.0g;Carbs: 3.0g.

Prawns With Mushrooms

Servings:4
Cooking Time:25 Minutes
Ingredients:

- 1 lb tiger prawns, peeled and deveined
- 3 tbsp olive oil
- 2 green onions, sliced
- ½ lb white mushrooms, sliced
- 2 tbsp balsamic vinegar
- 2 tsp garlic, minced

Directions:

1. Warm the olive oil in a skillet over medium heat and cook green onions and garlic for 2 minutes. Stir in mushrooms and balsamic vinegar and cook for an additional 6 minutes. Put in prawns and cook for 4 minutes. Serve right away.

Nutrition Info:

- Info Per Serving: Calories: 260;Fat: 9g;Protein: 19g;Carbs: 13g.

Juicy Basil-tomato Scallops

Servings:4
Cooking Time:20 Minutes
Ingredients:

- 2 tbsp olive oil
- 1 tbsp basil, chopped
- 1 lb scallops, scrubbed
- 1 tbsp garlic, minced
- 1 onion, chopped
- 6 tomatoes, cubed
- 1 cup heavy cream
- 1 tbsp parsley, chopped

Directions:

1. Warm the olive oil in a skillet over medium heat and cook garlic and onion for 2 minutes. Stir in scallops, basil, tomatoes, heavy cream, and parsley and cook for an additional 7 minutes. Serve immediately.

Nutrition Info:

- Info Per Serving: Calories: 270;Fat: 12g;Protein: 11g;Carbs: 17g.

Pan-fried Tuna With Vegetables

Servings:4
Cooking Time:25 Minutes
Ingredients:
- 2 tbsp olive oil
- 4 tuna fillets, boneless
- 1 red bell pepper, chopped
- 1 onion, chopped
- 4 garlic cloves, minced
- ½ cup fish stock
- 1 tsp basil, dried
- ½ cup cherry tomatoes, halved
- ½ cup black olives, halved
- Salt and black pepper to taste

Directions:
1. Warm the olive oil in a skillet over medium heat and fry tuna for 10 minutes on both sides. Divide the fish among plates. In the same skillet, cook onion, bell pepper, garlic, and cherry tomatoes for 3 minutes. Stir in salt, pepper, fish stock, basil, and olives and cook for another 3 minutes. Top the tuna with the mixture and serve immediately.

Nutrition Info:
- Info Per Serving: Calories: 260;Fat: 9g;Protein: 29g;Carbs: 6g.

Parsley Tomato Tilapia

Servings:4
Cooking Time:20 Minutes
Ingredients:
- 2 tbsp olive oil
- 4 tilapia fillets, boneless
- ½ cup tomato sauce
- 2 tbsp parsley, chopped
- Salt and black pepper to taste

Directions:
1. Warm olive oil in a skillet over medium heat. Sprinkle tilapia with salt and pepper and cook until golden brown, flipping once, about 6 minutes. Pour in the tomato sauce and parsley and cook for an additional 4 minutes. Serve immediately.

Nutrition Info:
- Info Per Serving: Calories: 308;Fat: 17g;Protein: 16g;Carbs: 3g.

Dill Smoked Salmon & Eggplant Rolls

Servings:4
Cooking Time:20 Minutes
Ingredients:
- 2 eggplants, lengthwise cut into thin slices
- 2 tbsp olive oil
- 1 cup ricotta cheese, soft
- 4 oz smoked salmon, chopped
- 2 tsp lemon zest, grated
- 1 small red onion, sliced
- Salt and pepper to the taste

Directions:
1. Mix salmon, cheese, lemon zest, onion, salt, and pepper in a bowl. Grease the eggplant with olive oil and grill them on a preheated grill pan for 3-4 minutes per side. Set aside to cool. Spread the cooled eggplant slices with the salmon mixture. Roll out and secure with toothpicks and serve.

Nutrition Info:
- Info Per Serving: Calories: 310;Fat: 25g;Protein: 12g;Carbs: 16g.

Mediterranean Grilled Sea Bass

Servings:6
Cooking Time: 20 Minutes
Ingredients:

- ¼ teaspoon onion powder
- ¼ teaspoon garlic powder
- ¼ teaspoon paprika
- Lemon pepper and sea salt to taste
- 2 pounds sea bass
- 3 tablespoons extra-virgin olive oil, divided
- 2 large cloves garlic, chopped
- 1 tablespoon chopped Italian flat leaf parsley

Directions:

1. Preheat the grill to high heat.
2. Place the onion powder, garlic powder, paprika, lemon pepper, and sea salt in a large bowl and stir to combine.
3. Dredge the fish in the spice mixture, turning until well coated.
4. Heat 2 tablespoon of olive oil in a small skillet. Add the garlic and parsley and cook for 1 to 2 minutes, stirring occasionally. Remove the skillet from the heat and set aside.
5. Brush the grill grates lightly with remaining 1 tablespoon olive oil.
6. Grill the fish for about 7 minutes. Flip the fish and drizzle with the garlic mixture and cook for an additional 7 minutes, or until the fish flakes when pressed lightly with a fork.
7. Serve hot.

Nutrition Info:

- Info Per Serving: Calories: 200;Fat: 10.3g;Protein: 26.9g;Carbs: 0.6g.

Salmon And Mushroom Hash With Pesto

Servings:6
Cooking Time: 20 Minutes
Ingredients:

- Pesto:
- ¼ cup extra-virgin olive oil
- 1 bunch fresh basil
- Juice and zest of 1 lemon
- ⅓ cup water
- ¼ teaspoon salt, plus additional as needed
- Hash:
- 2 tablespoons extra-virgin olive oil
- 6 cups mixed mushrooms (brown, white, shiitake, cremini, portobello, etc.), sliced
- 1 pound wild salmon, cubed

Directions:

1. Make the pesto: Pulse the olive oil, basil, juice and zest, water, and salt in a blender or food processor until smoothly blended. Set aside.
2. Heat the olive oil in a large skillet over medium heat.
3. Stir-fry the mushrooms for 6 to 8 minutes, or until they begin to exude their juices.
4. Add the salmon and cook each side for 5 to 6 minutes until cooked through.
5. Fold in the prepared pesto and stir well. Taste and add additional salt as needed. Serve warm.

Nutrition Info:

- Info Per Serving: Calories: 264;Fat: 14.7g;Protein: 7.0g;Carbs: 30.9g.

Dill Baked Sea Bass

Servings:6
Cooking Time: 10 To 15 Minutes
Ingredients:

- ¼ cup olive oil
- 2 pounds sea bass
- Sea salt and freshly ground pepper, to taste
- 1 garlic clove, minced
- ¼ cup dry white wine
- 3 teaspoons fresh dill
- 2 teaspoons fresh thyme

Directions:

1. Preheat the oven to 425°F.
2. Brush the bottom of a roasting pan with the olive oil. Place the fish in the pan and brush the fish with oil.
3. Season the fish with sea salt and freshly ground pepper. Combine the remaining ingredients and pour over the fish.
4. Bake in the preheated oven for 10 to 15 minutes, depending on the size of the fish.
5. Serve hot.

Nutrition Info:

- Info Per Serving: Calories: 224;Fat: 12.1g;Protein: 28.1g;Carbs: 0.9g.

Parchment Orange & Dill Salmon

Servings:4
Cooking Time:25 Minutes
Ingredients:

- 2 tbsp butter, melted
- 4 salmon fillets
- Salt and black pepper to taste
- 1 orange, juiced and zested
- 4 tbsp fresh dill, chopped

Directions:

1. Preheat oven to 375 °F. Coat the salmon fillets on both sides with butter. Season with salt and pepper and divide them between 4 pieces of parchment paper. Drizzle the orange juice over each piece of fish and top with orange zest and dill. Wrap the paper around the fish to make packets. Place on a baking sheet and bake for 15-20 minutes until the cod is cooked through. Serve and enjoy!

Nutrition Info:

- Info Per Serving: Calories: 481;Fat: 21g;Protein: 65g;Carbs: 4.2g.

Avocado & Onion Tilapia

Servings:4
Cooking Time:10 Minutes
Ingredients:

- 1 tbsp olive oil
- 1 tbsp orange juice
- ¼ tsp kosher salt
- ½ tsp ground coriander seeds
- 4 tilapia fillets, skin-on
- ¼ cup chopped red onions
- 1 avocado, skinned and sliced

Directions:

1. In a bowl, mix together the olive oil, orange juice, ground coriander seeds, and salt. Add the fish and turn to coat on all sides. Arrange the fillets on a greased microwave-safe dish. Top with onion and cover the dish with plastic wrap, leaving a small part open at the edge to vent the steam. Microwave on high for about 3 minutes. The fish is done when it just begins to separate into chunks when pressed gently with a fork. Top the fillets with the avocado and serve.

Nutrition Info:

- Info Per Serving: Calories: 210;Fat: 11g;Protein: 25g;Carbs: 5g.

Hake Fillet In Herby Tomato Sauce

Servings:4
Cooking Time:30 Minutes
Ingredients:
- 2 tbsp olive oil
- 1 onion, sliced thin
- 1 fennel bulb, sliced
- Salt and black pepper to taste
- 4 garlic cloves, minced
- 1 tsp fresh thyme, chopped
- 1 can diced tomatoes,
- ½ cup dry white wine
- 4 skinless hake fillets
- 2 tbsp fresh basil, chopped

Directions:
1. Warm the olive oil in a skillet over medium heat. Sauté the onion and fennel for about 5 minutes until softened. Stir in garlic and thyme and cook for about 30 seconds until fragrant. Pour in tomatoes and wine and bring to simmer.
2. Season the hake with salt and pepper. Nestle hake skinned side down into the tomato sauce and spoon some sauce over the top. Bring to simmer. Cook for 10-12 minutes until hake easily flakes with a fork. Sprinkle with basil and serve.

Nutrition Info:
- Info Per Serving: Calories: 452;Fat: 9.9g;Protein: 78g;Carbs: 9.7g.

Shrimp & Salmon In Tomato Sauce

Servings:4
Cooking Time:30 Minutes
Ingredients:
- 1 lb shrimp, peeled and deveined
- 2 tbsp olive oil
- 1 lb salmon fillets
- Salt and black pepper to taste
- 1 cups tomatoes, chopped
- 1 onion, chopped
- 2 garlic cloves, minced
- ¼ tsp red pepper flakes
- 1 cup fish stock
- 1 tbsp cilantro, chopped

Directions:
1. Preheat the oven to 360°F. Line a baking sheet with parchment paper. Season the salmon with salt and pepper, drizzle with some olive oil, and arrange them on the sheet. Bake for 15 minutes. Remove to a serving plate.
2. Warm the remaining olive oil in a skillet over medium heat and sauté onion and garlic for 3 minutes until tender. Pour in tomatoes, fish stock, salt, pepper, and red pepper flakes and bring to a boil. Simmer for 10 minutes. Stir in shrimp and cook for another 8 minutes. Pour the sauce over the salmon and serve sprinkled with cilantro.

Nutrition Info:
- Info Per Serving: Calories: 240;Fat: 16g;Protein: 18g;Carbs: 22g.

Shrimp And Pea Paella

Servings:2
Cooking Time: 60 Minutes
Ingredients:

- 2 tablespoons olive oil
- 1 garlic clove, minced
- ½ large onion, minced
- 1 cup diced tomato
- ½ cup short-grain rice
- ½ teaspoon sweet paprika
- ½ cup dry white wine
- 1¼ cups low-sodium chicken stock
- 8 ounces large raw shrimp
- 1 cup frozen peas
- ¼ cup jarred roasted red peppers, cut into strips
- Salt, to taste

Directions:

1. Heat the olive oil in a large skillet over medium-high heat.
2. Add the garlic and onion and sauté for 3 minutes, or until the onion is softened.
3. Add the tomato, rice, and paprika and stir for 3 minutes to toast the rice.
4. Add the wine and chicken stock and stir to combine. Bring the mixture to a boil.
5. Cover and reduce the heat to medium-low, and simmer for 45 minutes, or until the rice is just about tender and most of the liquid has been absorbed.
6. Add the shrimp, peas, and roasted red peppers. Cover and cook for an additional 5 minutes. Season with salt to taste and serve.

Nutrition Info:

- Info Per Serving: Calories: 646;Fat: 27.1g;Protein: 42.0g;Carbs: 59.7g.

Cheesy Smoked Salmon Crostini

Servings:4
Cooking Time:10 Min + Chilling Time
Ingredients:

- 4 oz smoked salmon, sliced
- 2 oz feta cheese, crumbled
- 4 oz cream cheese, softened
- 2 tbsp horseradish sauce
- 2 tsp orange zest
- 1 red onion, chopped
- 2 tbsp chives, chopped
- 1 baguette, sliced and toasted

Directions:

1. In a bowl, mix cream cheese, horseradish sauce, onion, feta cheese, and orange zest until smooth. Spread the mixture on the baguette slices. Top with salmon and chives to serve.

Nutrition Info:

- Info Per Serving: Calories: 290;Fat: 19g;Protein: 26g;Carbs: 5g.

Roasted Cod With Cabbage

Servings:4
Cooking Time:30 Minutes
Ingredients:

- 2 tbsp olive oil
- 1 head white cabbage, shredded
- 1 tsp garlic powder
- 1 tsp smoked paprika
- 4 cod fillets, boneless
- ½ cup tomato sauce
- 1 tsp Italian seasoning
- 1 tbsp chives, chopped

Directions:

1. Preheat the oven to 390°F. Mix cabbage, garlic powder, paprika, olive oil, tomato sauce, Italian seasoning, and chives in a roasting pan. Top with cod fillets and bake covered with foil for 20 minutes. Serve immediately.

Nutrition Info:

- Info Per Serving: Calories: 200;Fat: 14g;Protein: 18g;Carbs: 24g.

Baked Haddock With Rosemary Gremolata

Servings:6
Cooking Time:35 Min + Marinating Time
Ingredients:

- 1 cup milk
- Salt and black pepper to taste
- 2 tbsp rosemary, chopped
- 1 garlic clove, minced
- 1 lemon, zested
- 1 ½ lb haddock fillets

Directions:
1. In a large bowl, coat the fish with milk, salt, pepper, and 1 tablespoon of rosemary. Refrigerate for 2 hours.
2. Preheat oven to 380ºF. Carefully remove the haddock from the marinade, drain thoroughly, and place in a greased baking dish. Cover and bake 15–20 minutes until the fish is flaky. Remove fish from the oven and let it rest 5 minutes. To make the gremolata, mix the remaining rosemary, lemon zest, and garlic. Sprinkle the fish with gremolata and serve.

Nutrition Info:
- Info Per Serving: Calories: 112;Fat: 2g;Protein: 20g;Carbs: 3g.

Asian-inspired Tuna Lettuce Wraps

Servings:2
Cooking Time: 0 Minutes
Ingredients:

- ⅓ cup almond butter
- 1 tablespoon freshly squeezed lemon juice
- 1 teaspoon low-sodium soy sauce
- 1 teaspoon curry powder
- ½ teaspoon sriracha, or to taste
- ½ cup canned water chestnuts, drained and chopped
- 2 package tuna packed in water, drained
- 2 large butter lettuce leaves

Directions:
1. Stir together the almond butter, lemon juice, soy sauce, curry powder, sriracha in a medium bowl until well mixed. Add the water chestnuts and tuna and stir until well incorporated.
2. Place 2 butter lettuce leaves on a flat work surface, spoon half of the tuna mixture onto each leaf and roll up into a wrap. Serve immediately.

Nutrition Info:
- Info Per Serving: Calories: 270;Fat: 13.9g;Protein: 19.1g;Carbs: 18.5g.

Seafood Cakes With Radicchio Salad

Servings:4
Cooking Time:30 Minutes
Ingredients:

- 2 tbsp butter
- 2 tbsp extra-virgin olive oil
- 1 lb lump crabmeat
- 4 scallions, sliced
- 1 garlic clove, minced
- ¼ cup cooked shrimp
- 2 tbsp heavy cream
- ¼ head radicchio, thinly sliced
- 1 green apple, shredded
- 2 tbsp lemon juice
- Salt and black pepper to taste

Directions:
1. In a food processor, place the shrimp, heavy cream, salt, and pepper. Blend until smooth. Mix crab meat and scallions in a bowl. Add in shrimp mixture and toss to combine. Make 4 patties out of the mixture. Transfer to the fridge for 10 minutes. Warm butter in a skillet over medium heat and brown patties for 8 minutes on all sides. Remove to a serving plate. Mix radicchio and apple in a bowl. Combine olive oil, lemon juice, garlic, and salt in a small bowl and stir well. Pour over the salad and toss to combine. Serve and enjoy!

Nutrition Info:
- Info Per Serving: Calories: 238;Fat: 14.3g;Protein: 20g;Carbs: 8g.

Herby Mackerel Fillets In Red Sauce

Servings:2
Cooking Time:15 Minutes
Ingredients:
- 1 tbsp butter
- 2 mackerel fillets
- ¼ cup white wine
- ½ cup spring onions, sliced
- 2 garlic cloves, minced
- ½ tsp dried thyme
- 1 tsp dried parsley
- Salt and black pepper to taste
- ½ cup vegetable broth
- ½ cup tomato sauce
- ½ tsp hot sauce
- 1 tbsp fresh mint, chopped

Directions:
1. In a pot over medium heat, melt the butter. Add in fish and cook for 6 minutes in total; set aside. Pour in the wine and scrape off any bits from the bottom. Add in spring onions and garlic; cook for 3 minutes until fragrant. Sprinkle with thyme, parsley, salt, and pepper. Stir in vegetable broth, tomato sauce, and add back the fillets. Cook for 3-4 minutes. Stir in hot sauce and top with mint. Serve and enjoy!

Nutrition Info:
- Info Per Serving: Calories: 334;Fat: 22g;Protein: 23.8g;Carbs: 7g.

Baked Fish With Pistachio Crust

Servings:4
Cooking Time: 15 To 20 Minutes
Ingredients:
- ½ cup extra-virgin olive oil, divided
- 1 pound flaky white fish (such as cod, haddock, or halibut), skin removed
- ½ cup shelled finely chopped pistachios
- ½ cup ground flaxseed
- Zest and juice of 1 lemon, divided
- 1 teaspoon ground cumin
- 1 teaspoon ground allspice
- ½ teaspoon salt
- ¼ teaspoon freshly ground black pepper

Directions:
1. Preheat the oven to 400ºF.
2. Line a baking sheet with parchment paper or aluminum foil and drizzle 2 tablespoons of olive oil over the sheet, spreading to evenly coat the bottom.
3. Cut the fish into 4 equal pieces and place on the prepared baking sheet.
4. In a small bowl, combine the pistachios, flaxseed, lemon zest, cumin, allspice, salt, and pepper. Drizzle in ¼ cup of olive oil and stir well.
5. Divide the nut mixture evenly on top of the fish pieces. Drizzle the lemon juice and remaining 2 tablespoons of olive oil over the fish and bake until cooked through, 15 to 20 minutes, depending on the thickness of the fish.
6. Cool for 5 minutes before serving.

Nutrition Info:
- Info Per Serving: Calories: 509;Fat: 41.0g;Protein: 26.0g;Carbs: 9.0g.

Pan-fried Chili Sea Scallops

Servings:4

Cooking Time:25 Minutes

Ingredients:

- 1 ½ lb large sea scallops, tendons removed
- 3 tbsp olive oil
- 1 garlic clove, finely chopped
- ½ red pepper flakes
- 2 tbsp chili sauce
- ¼ cup tomato sauce
- 1 small shallot, minced
- 1 tbsp minced fresh cilantro
- Salt and black pepper to taste

Directions:

1. Warm the olive oil in a skillet over medium heat. Add the scallops and cook for 2 minutes without moving them. Flip them and continue to cook for 2 more minutes, without moving them, until golden browned. Set aside. Add the shallot and garlic to the skillet and sauté for 3-5 minutes until softened. Pour in the chili sauce, tomato sauce, and red pepper flakes and stir for 3-4 minutes. Add the scallops back and warm through. Adjust the taste and top with cilantro.

Nutrition Info:

- Info Per Serving: Calories: 204;Fat: 14.1g;Protein: 14g;Carbs: 5g.

Rosemary Wine Poached Haddock

Servings:4

Cooking Time:40 Minutes

Ingredients:

- 4 haddock fillets
- Salt and black pepper to taste
- 2 garlic cloves, minced
- ½ cup dry white wine
- ½ cup seafood stock
- 4 rosemary sprigs for garnish

Directions:

1. Preheat oven to 380 °F. Sprinkle haddock fillets with salt and black pepper and arrange them on a baking dish. Pour in the wine, garlic, and stock. Bake covered for 20 minutes until the fish is tender; remove to a serving plate. Pour the cooking liquid into a pot over high heat. Cook for 10 minutes until reduced by half. Place on serving dishes and top with the reduced poaching liquid. Serve garnished with rosemary.

Nutrition Info:

- Info Per Serving: Calories: 215;Fat: 4g;Protein: 35g;Carbs: 3g.

Poultry And Meats Recipes

Potato Lamb And Olive Stew

Servings:10
Cooking Time: 3 Hours 42 Minutes
Ingredients:

- 4 tablespoons almond flour
- ¾ cup low-sodium chicken stock
- 1¼ pounds small potatoes, halved
- 3 cloves garlic, minced
- 4 large shallots, cut into ½-inch wedges
- 3 sprigs fresh rosemary
- 1 tablespoon lemon zest
- Coarse sea salt and black pepper, to taste
- 3½ pounds lamb shanks, fat trimmed and cut crosswise into 1½-inch pieces
- 2 tablespoons extra-virgin olive oil
- ½ cup dry white wine
- 1 cup pitted green olives, halved
- 2 tablespoons lemon juice

Directions:

1. Combine 1 tablespoon of almond flour with chicken stock in a bowl. Stir to mix well.
2. Put the flour mixture, potatoes, garlic, shallots, rosemary, and lemon zest in the slow cooker. Sprinkle with salt and black pepper. Stir to mix well. Set aside.
3. Combine the remaining almond flour with salt and black pepper in a large bowl, then dunk the lamb shanks in the flour and toss to coat.
4. Heat the olive oil in a nonstick skillet over medium-high heat until shimmering.
5. Add the well-coated lamb and cook for 10 minutes or until golden brown. Flip the lamb pieces halfway through the cooking time. Transfer the cooked lamb to the slow cooker.
6. Pour the wine in the same skillet, then cook for 2 minutes or until it reduces in half. Pour the wine in the slow cooker.
7. Put the slow cooker lid on and cook on high for 3 hours and 30 minutes or until the lamb is very tender.
8. In the last 20 minutes of the cooking, open the lid and fold in the olive halves to cook.
9. Pour the stew on a large plate, let them sit for 5 minutes, then skim any fat remains over the face of the liquid.
10. Drizzle with lemon juice and sprinkle with salt and pepper. Serve warm.

Nutrition Info:

- Info Per Serving: Calories: 309;Fat: 10.3g;Protein: 36.9g;Carbs: 16.1g.

Chicken Drumsticks With Peach Glaze

Servings:4
Cooking Time:35 Minutes
Ingredients:

- 2 tbsp olive oil
- 8 chicken drumsticks, skinless
- 3 peaches, peeled and chopped
- ¼ cup honey
- ¼ cup cider vinegar
- 1 sweet onion, chopped
- 1 tsp minced fresh rosemary
- Salt to taste

Directions:

1. Warm the olive oil in a large skillet over medium heat. Sprinkle chicken with salt and pepper and brown it for about 7 minutes per side. Remove to a plate. Add onion and rosemary to the skillet and sauté for 1 minute or until lightly golden. Add honey, vinegar, salt, and peaches and cook for 10-12 minutes or until peaches are softened. Add the chicken back to the skillet and heat just until warm, brushing with the sauce. Serve chicken thighs with peach sauce. Enjoy!

Nutrition Info:

- Info Per Serving: Calories: 1492;Fat: 26g;Protein: 54g;Carbs: 27g.

Deluxe Chicken With Yogurt Sauce

Servings:4
Cooking Time:40 Minutes
Ingredients:

- 2 tbsp olive oil
- 1/3 cup Greek yogurt
- 1 lb chicken breasts, halved
- 2 garlic cloves, minced
- 2 tbsp lemon juice
- 1 tbsp red wine vinegar
- 2 tbsp dill, chopped
- Salt and black pepper to taste

Directions:

1. Preheat the oven to 380° F. In a food processor, blend garlic, lemon juice, vinegar, yogurt, dill, salt, and pepper until smooth. Warm olive oil in a skillet over medium heat. Sear chicken for 6 minutes on both sides. Pour yogurt sauce over chicken and bake for 25 minutes. Serve.

Nutrition Info:

- Info Per Serving: Calories: 290;Fat: 13g;Protein: 15g;Carbs: 19g.

Pork Chops In Tomato Olive Sauce

Servings:4
Cooking Time:20 Minutes
Ingredients:

- 2 tbsp olive oil
- 4 pork loin chops, boneless
- 6 tomatoes, crushed
- 3 tbsp basil, chopped
- 10 black olives, halved
- 1 yellow onion, chopped
- 1 garlic clove, minced

Directions:

1. Warm the olive oil in a skillet over medium heat and brown pork chops for 6 minutes on all sides. Share into plates. In the same skillet, stir tomatoes, basil, olives, onion, and garlic and simmer for 4 minutes. Drizzle tomato sauce over.

Nutrition Info:

- Info Per Serving: Calories: 340;Fat: 18g;Protein: 35g;Carbs: 13g.

Asparagus & Chicken Skillet

Servings:4
Cooking Time:30 Minutes
Ingredients:

- 2 tbsp olive oil
- 1 lb chicken breasts, sliced
- Salt and black pepper to taste
- 1 lb asparagus, chopped
- 6 sundried tomatoes, diced
- 3 tbsp capers, drained
- 2 tbsp lemon juice

Directions:

1. Warm the olive oil in a skillet over medium heat. Cook asparagus, tomatoes, salt, pepper, capers, and lemon juice for 10 minutes. Remove to a bowl. Brown chicken in the same skillet for 8 minutes on both sides. Put veggies back to skillet and cook for another 2-3 minutes. Serve and enjoy!

Nutrition Info:

- Info Per Serving: Calories: 560;Fat: 29g;Protein: 45g;Carbs: 34g.

Chicken Sausage & Zucchini Soup

Servings:4
Cooking Time:30 Minutes
Ingredients:

- 2 tbsp olive oil
- 2 chicken sausage, chopped
- 4 cups chicken stock
- 3 garlic cloves, minced
- 1 yellow onion, chopped
- 4 zucchinis, cubed
- 1 lemon, zested
- ½ cup basil, chopped
- Salt and black pepper to taste

Directions:
1. Warm the olive oil in a pot over medium heat and brown the sausages for 5 minutes; reserve. Add zucchini, onion, and garlic to the pot and sauté for 5 minutes. Add in the chicken stock, lemon zest, salt, and pepper and bring to a boil. Simmer for 10 minutes. Return the sausages and cook for another 5 minutes. Top with basil and serve right away.

Nutrition Info:

- Info Per Serving: Calories: 280;Fat: 12g;Protein: 5g;Carbs: 17g.

Sweet Chicken Stew

Servings:4
Cooking Time:50 Minutes
Ingredients:

- 2 tbsp olive oil
- 3 garlic cloves, minced
- 3 tbsp cilantro, chopped
- Salt and black pepper to taste
- 2 cups chicken stock
- 2 shallots, thinly sliced
- 1 lb chicken breasts, cubed
- 5 oz dried pitted prunes, halved

Directions:
1. Warm the olive oil in a pot over medium heat and cook shallots and garlic for 3 minutes. Add in chicken breasts and cook for another 5 minutes, stirring occasionally. Pour in chicken stock and prunes and season with salt and pepper. Cook for 30 minutes. Garnish with cilantro and serve.

Nutrition Info:

- Info Per Serving: Calories: 310;Fat: 26g;Protein: 7g;Carbs: 16g.

Panko Grilled Chicken Patties

Servings:4
Cooking Time: 8 To 10 Minutes
Ingredients:

- 1 pound ground chicken
- 3 tablespoons crumbled feta cheese
- 3 tablespoons finely chopped red pepper
- ¼ cup finely chopped red onion
- 3 tablespoons panko bread crumbs
- 1 garlic clove, minced
- 1 teaspoon chopped fresh oregano
- ¼ teaspoon salt
- ⅛ teaspoon freshly ground black pepper
- Cooking spray

Directions:
1. Mix together the ground chicken, feta cheese, red pepper, red onion, bread crumbs, garlic, oregano, salt, and black pepper in a large bowl, and stir to incorporate.
2. Divide the chicken mixture into 8 equal portions and form each portion into a patty with your hands.
3. Preheat a grill to medium-high heat and oil the grill grates with cooking spray.
4. Arrange the patties on the grill grates and grill each side for 4 to 5 minutes, or until the patties are cooked through.
5. Rest for 5 minutes before serving.

Nutrition Info:

- Info Per Serving: Calories: 241;Fat: 13.5g;Protein: 23.2g;Carbs: 6.7g.

Chicken & Vegetable Skewers

Servings:6
Cooking Time:20 Minutes
Ingredients:

- 2 tbsp olive oil
- 1 ½ lb chicken breasts, cubed
- 1 tbsp fresh chives, chopped
- 1 zucchini, sliced thick
- 1 tbsp Italian seasoning
- 1 cup bell peppers, sliced
- 1 red onion, cut into wedges
- 1 ½ cups cherry tomatoes

Directions:

1. Preheat grill to high. Toss the chicken cubes with olive oil and Italian seasoning. Thread them onto skewers, alternating with the vegetables. Grill the skewers for 10 minutes, turning them occasionally to ensure even cooking. Top with chives.

Nutrition Info:

- Info Per Serving: Calories: 295;Fat: 14g;Protein: 36g;Carbs: 6g.

Cocktail Meatballs In Almond Sauce

Servings:4
Cooking Time:30 Minutes
Ingredients:

- 3 tbsp olive oil
- 8 oz ground pork
- 8 oz ground beef
- ½ cup finely minced onions
- 1 large egg, beaten
- 1 potato, shredded
- Salt and black pepper to taste
- 1 tsp garlic powder
- ½ tsp oregano
- 2 tbsp chopped parsley
- ¼ cup ground almonds
- 1 cup chicken broth
- ¼ cup butter

Directions:

1. Place the ground meat, onions, egg, potato, salt, garlic powder, pepper, and oregano in a large bowl. Shape the mixture into small meatballs, about 1 inch in diameter, and place on a plate. Let sit for 10 minutes at room temperature.
2. Warm the olive oil in a skillet over medium heat. Add the meatballs and brown them for 6-8 minutes on all sides; reserve. In the hot skillet, melt the butter and add the almonds and broth. Cook for 3-5 minutes. Add the meatballs to the skillet, cover, and cook for 8-10 minutes. Top with parsley.

Nutrition Info:

- Info Per Serving: Calories: 449;Fat: 42g;Protein: 16g;Carbs: 3g.

Rosemary Pork Loin With Green Onions

Servings:4
Cooking Time:50 Minutes
Ingredients:

- 2 lb pork loin roast, boneless and cubed
- 2 tbsp olive oil
- 2 garlic cloves, minced
- Salt and black pepper to taste
- 1 cup tomato sauce
- 1 tsp rosemary, chopped
- 4 green onions, chopped

Directions:

1. Preheat the oven to 360° F. Heat olive oil in a skillet over medium heat and cook pork, garlic, and green onions for 6-7 minutes, stirring often. Add in tomato sauce, rosemary, and 1 cup of water. Season with salt and pepper. Transfer to a baking dish and bake for 40 minutes. Serve warm.

Nutrition Info:

- Info Per Serving: Calories: 280;Fat: 16g;Protein: 19g;Carbs: 18g.

Chicken With Halloumi Cheese

Servings:4
Cooking Time:40 Minutes
Ingredients:

- 2 tbsp butter
- 1 cup Halloumi cheese, cubed
- Salt and black pepper to taste
- 1 hard-boiled egg yolk
- ½ cup olive oil
- 6 black olives, halved
- 1 tbsp fresh cilantro, chopped
- 1 tbsp balsamic vinegar
- 1 tbsp garlic, finely minced
- 1 tbsp fresh lemon juice
- 1 ½ lb chicken wings

Directions:

1. Melt the butter in a saucepan over medium heat. Sear the chicken wings for 5 minutes per side. Season with salt and pepper to taste. Place the chicken wings on a parchment-lined baking pan. Mash the egg yolk with a fork and mix in the garlic, lemon juice, balsamic vinegar, olive oil, and salt until creamy, uniform, and smooth.
2. Preheat oven to 380° F. Spread the egg mixture over the chicken. Bake for 15-20 minutes. Top with the cheese and bake an additional 5 minutes until hot and bubbly. Scatter cilantro and olives on top of the chicken wings. Serve.

Nutrition Info:

- Info Per Serving: Calories: 560;Fat: 48g;Protein: 41g;Carbs: 2g.

Peppery Chicken Bake

Servings:4
Cooking Time:70 Minutes
Ingredients:

- 3 tbsp olive oil
- 1 lb chicken breasts, sliced
- 2 lb cherry tomatoes, halved
- 1 onion, chopped
- 3 garlic cloves, minced
- 3 red chili peppers, chopped
- ½ lemon, zested
- Salt and black pepper to taste

Directions:

1. Warm the olive oil in a skillet over medium heat and brown chicken for 8 minutes on both sides. Remove to a roasting pan. In the same skillet, add onion, garlic, and chili peppers and cook for 2 minutes. Pour the mixture over the chicken and toss to coat. Add in tomatoes, lemon zest, 1 cup of water, salt, and pepper. Bake for 45 minutes. Serve and enjoy!

Nutrition Info:

- Info Per Serving: Calories: 280;Fat: 14g;Protein: 34g;Carbs: 25g.

Paprika Chicken With Caper Dressing

Servings:4
Cooking Time:35 Minutes
Ingredients:

- 2 tbsp canola oil
- 4 chicken breast halves
- Salt and black pepper to taste
- 1 tbsp sweet paprika
- 1 onion, chopped
- 1 tbsp balsamic vinegar
- 2 tbsp parsley, chopped
- 1 avocado, peeled and cubed
- 2 tbsp capers

Directions:

1. Preheat the grill over medium heat. Rub chicken halves with half of the canola oil, paprika, salt, and pepper and grill them for 14 minutes on both sides. Share into plates. Combine onion, remaining oil, vinegar, parsley, avocado, and capers in a bowl. Pour the sauce over the chicken and serve.

Nutrition Info:

- Info Per Serving: Calories: 300;Fat: 13g;Protein: 15g;Carbs: 25g.

Chicken Souvlaki

Servings:4
Cooking Time:20 Min + Cooling Time
Ingredients:

- 1 red bell pepper, cut into chunks
- 2 chicken breasts, cubed
- 2 tbsp olive oil
- 2 cloves garlic, minced
- 8 oz cipollini onions
- ½ cup lemon juice
- Salt and black pepper to taste
- 1 tsp rosemary, chopped
- 1 cup tzatziki sauce

Directions:

1. In a bowl, mix oil, garlic, salt, pepper, and lemon juice and add the chicken, cipollini, rosemary, and bell pepper. Refrigerate for 2 hours. Preheat your grill to high heat. Thread chicken, bell pepper, and cipollini onto skewers and grill them for 6 minutes per side. Serve with tzatziki sauce.

Nutrition Info:

- Info Per Serving: Calories: 363;Fat: 14.1g;Protein: 32g;Carbs: 8g.

Nutty Chicken Breasts

Servings:4
Cooking Time:65 Minutes
Ingredients:

- 2 tbsp canola oil
- 1 lb chicken breasts, halved
- ½ tsp hot paprika
- 1 cup chicken stock
- 2 tbsp hazelnuts, chopped
- 2 spring onions, chopped
- 2 garlic cloves, minced
- ¼ cup Parmesan cheese, grated
- 2 tbsp cilantro, chopped
- 2 tbsp parsley, chopped
- Salt and black pepper to taste

Directions:

1. Preheat the oven to 370° F. Combine chicken, canola oil, hot paprika, stock, hazelnuts, spring onions, garlic, salt, and pepper in a greased baking pan and bake for 40 minutes. Sprinkle with Parmesan cheese and bake for an additional 5 minutes until the cheese melts. Top with cilantro and parsley.

Nutrition Info:

- Info Per Serving: Calories: 230;Fat: 10g;Protein: 19g;Carbs: 22g.

Marjoram Pork Loin With Ricotta Cheese

Servings:4
Cooking Time:70 Minutes
Ingredients:

- 2 tbsp olive oil
- 1 ½ lb pork loin, cubed
- 2 tbsp marjoram, chopped
- 1 garlic clove, minced
- 1 tbsp capers, drained
- 1 cup chicken stock
- Salt and black pepper to taste
- ½ cup ricotta cheese, crumbled

Directions:

1. Warm olive oil in a skillet over medium heat and sear pork for 5 minutes. Stir in marjoram, garlic, capers, stock, salt, and pepper and bring to a boil. Cook for 30 minutes. Mix in cheese.

Nutrition Info:

- Info Per Serving: Calories: 310;Fat: 15g;Protein: 34g;Carbs: 17g.

Juicy Pork Chops

Servings:4
Cooking Time:30 Minutes
Ingredients:

- 3 tbsp olive oil
- 4 pork chops
- Salt and black pepper to taste
- 5 tbsp chicken broth
- 6 garlic cloves, minced
- ¼ cup honey
- 2 tbsp apple cider vinegar
- 2 tbsp parsley, chopped

Directions:
1. Warm the olive oil in a large skillet over medium heat. Season the pork chops with salt and pepper and add them to the skillet. Cook for 10 minutes on both sides or until golden brown; reserve. Lower the heat and add 3 tablespoons of broth, scraping the bits and flavors from the bottom of the skillet; cook for 2 minutes until the broth evaporates. Add the garlic and cook for 30 seconds. Stir in honey, vinegar, and the remaining broth. Cook for 3-4 minutes until the sauce thickens slightly. Return the pork chops and cook for 2 minutes. Top with parsley and serve.

Nutrition Info:
- Info Per Serving: Calories: 302;Fat: 16g;Protein: 22g;Carbs: 19g.

Chicken With Bell Peppers

Servings:4
Cooking Time:65 Minutes
Ingredients:

- 2 tbsp olive oil
- 2 lb chicken breasts, cubed
- 2 garlic cloves, minced
- 1 red onion, chopped
- 2 red bell peppers, chopped
- ¼ tsp cumin, ground
- 2 cups corn
- ½ cup chicken stock
- 1 tsp chili powder

Directions:
1. Warm the olive oil in a skillet over medium heat and sear chicken for 8 minutes on both sides. Put in onion and garlic and cook for another 5 minutes. Stir in bell peppers, cumin, corn, stock, and chili powder. Cook for 45 minutes. Serve.

Nutrition Info:
- Info Per Serving: Calories: 340;Fat: 17g;Protein: 19g;Carbs: 27g.

Rich Beef Meal

Servings:4
Cooking Time:40 Minutes
Ingredients:

- 1 tbsp olive oil
- 1 lb beef meat, cubed
- 1 red onion, chopped
- 1 garlic clove, minced
- 1 celery stalk, chopped
- Salt and black pepper to taste
- 14 oz canned tomatoes, diced
- 1 cup vegetable stock
- ½ tsp ground nutmeg
- 2 tsp dill, chopped

Directions:
1. Warm the olive oil in a skillet over medium heat and cook onion and garlic for 5 minutes. Put in beef and cook for 5 more minutes. Stir in celery, salt, pepper, tomatoes, stock, nutmeg, and dill and bring to a boil. Cook for 20 minutes.

Nutrition Info:
- Info Per Serving: Calories: 300;Fat: 14g;Protein: 19g;Carbs: 16g.

Portuguese-style Chicken Breasts

Servings:4
Cooking Time:45 Minutes
Ingredients:

- 2 tbsp avocado oil
- 1 lb chicken breasts, cubed
- Salt and black pepper to taste
- 1 red onion, chopped
- 15 oz canned chickpeas
- 15 oz canned tomatoes, diced
- 1 cup Kalamata olives, pitted and halved
- 2 tbsp lime juice
- 1 tsp cilantro, chopped

Directions:

1. Warm the olive oil in a pot over medium heat and sauté chicken and onion for 5 minutes. Put in salt, pepper, chickpeas, tomatoes, olives, lime juice, cilantro, and 2 cups of water. Cover with lid and bring to a boil, then reduce the heat and simmer for 30 minutes. Serve warm.

Nutrition Info:

- Info Per Serving: Calories: 360;Fat: 16g;Protein: 28g;Carbs: 26g.

Greek Roasted Lamb Leg With Potatoes

Servings:6
Cooking Time:3 Hours 10 Minutes
Ingredients:

- 3 lb red potatoes, cut into 1-inch chunks
- 1 leg of lamb
- 2 tbsp olive oil
- 1 lemon, juiced
- 1 tsp dried Greek oregano
- ½ tsp dried rosemary
- 2 garlic cloves, minced
- Salt and black pepper to taste
- 3 tbsp butter, melted

Directions:

1. Preheat oven to 300° F. Season the lamb leg with oregano, rosemary, garlic, salt, and pepper and place it in a roasting pan, fat-side up. Brush with olive oil and sprinkle with some lemon juice. Bake for about 2 hours, brushing it occasionally.
2. Increase the oven temperature to 350° F. Spread the potatoes around the lamb. Season them with salt and pepper and drizzle with butter. Add ½ cup of water. Return the pan to the oven and roast for about 50-60 minutes until the lamb is cooked and the potatoes are tender. Remove, slice the lamb, and serve with the potatoes. Enjoy!

Nutrition Info:

- Info Per Serving: Calories: 770;Fat: 26g;Protein: 82g;Carbs: 42g.

Pork Chops In Wine Sauce

Servings:4
Cooking Time:30 Minutes
Ingredients:

- 2 tbsp olive oil
- 4 pork chops
- 1 cup red onion, sliced
- 10 black peppercorns, crushed
- ¼ cup vegetable stock
- ¼ cup dry white wine
- 2 garlic cloves, minced
- Salt to taste

Directions:

1. Warm the olive oil in a skillet over medium heat and sear pork chops for 8 minutes on both sides. Put in onion and garlic and cook for another 2 minutes. Mix in stock, wine, salt, and peppercorns and cook for 10 minutes, stirring often.

Nutrition Info:

- Info Per Serving: Calories: 240;Fat: 10g;Protein: 25g;Carbs: 14g.

Easy Grilled Pork Chops

Servings:4
Cooking Time: 10 Minutes
Ingredients:
- ¼ cup extra-virgin olive oil
- 2 tablespoons fresh thyme leaves
- 1 teaspoon smoked paprika
- 1 teaspoon salt
- 4 pork loin chops, ½-inch-thick

Directions:
1. In a small bowl, mix together the olive oil, thyme, paprika, and salt.
2. Put the pork chops in a plastic zip-top bag or a bowl and coat them with the spice mix. Let them marinate for 15 minutes.
3. Preheat the grill to high heat. Cook the pork chops for 4 minutes on each side until cooked through.
4. Serve warm.

Nutrition Info:
- Info Per Serving: Calories: 282;Fat: 23.0g;Protein: 21.0g;Carbs: 1.0g.

Greek-style Chicken & Egg Bake

Servings:4
Cooking Time:45 Minutes
Ingredients:
- ½ lb Halloumi cheese, grated
- 1 tbsp olive oil
- 1 lb chicken breasts, cubed
- 4 eggs, beaten
- 1 tsp dry mustard
- 2 cloves garlic, crushed
- 2 red bell peppers, sliced
- 1 red onion, sliced
- 2 tomatoes, chopped
- 1 tsp sweet paprika
- ½ tsp dried basil
- Salt to taste

Directions:
1. Preheat oven to 360° F. Warm the olive oil in a skillet over medium heat. Add the bell peppers, garlic, onion, and salt and cook for 3 minutes. Stir in tomatoes for an additional 5 minutes. Put in chicken breasts, paprika, dry mustard, and basil. Cook for another 6-8 minutes. Transfer the mixture to a greased baking pan and pour over the beaten eggs; season with salt. Bake for 15-18 minutes. Remove and spread the cheese over the top. Let cool for a few minutes. Serve sliced.

Nutrition Info:
- Info Per Serving: Calories: 480;Fat: 31g;Protein: 39g;Carbs: 12g.

Vegetable Mains And Meatless Recipes

Roasted Veggies And Brown Rice Bowl

Servings:4
Cooking Time: 20 Minutes
Ingredients:

- 2 cups cauliflower florets
- 2 cups broccoli florets
- 1 can chickpeas, drained and rinsed
- 1 cup carrot slices
- 2 to 3 tablespoons extra-virgin olive oil, divided
- Salt and freshly ground black pepper, to taste
- Nonstick cooking spray
- 2 cups cooked brown rice
- 2 to 3 tablespoons sesame seeds, for garnish
- Dressing:
- 3 to 4 tablespoons tahini
- 2 tablespoons honey
- 1 lemon, juiced
- 1 garlic clove, minced
- Salt and freshly ground black pepper, to taste

Directions:

1. Preheat the oven to 400ºF. Spritz two baking sheets with nonstick cooking spray.
2. Spread the cauliflower and broccoli on the first baking sheet and the second with the chickpeas and carrot slices.
3. Drizzle each sheet with half of the olive oil and sprinkle with salt and pepper. Toss to coat well.
4. Roast the chickpeas and carrot slices in the preheated oven for 10 minutes, leaving the carrots tender but crisp, and the cauliflower and broccoli for 20 minutes until fork-tender. Stir them once halfway through the cooking time.
5. Meanwhile, make the dressing: Whisk together the tahini, honey, lemon juice, garlic, salt, and pepper in a small bowl.
6. Divide the cooked brown rice among four bowls. Top each bowl evenly with roasted vegetables and dressing. Sprinkle the sesame seeds on top for garnish before serving.

Nutrition Info:

- Info Per Serving: Calories: 453;Fat: 17.8g;Protein: 12.1g;Carbs: 61.8g.

Vegan Lentil Bolognese

Servings:2
Cooking Time: 50 Minutes
Ingredients:

- 1 medium celery stalk
- 1 large carrot
- ½ large onion
- 1 garlic clove
- 2 tablespoons olive oil
- 1 can crushed tomatoes
- 1 cup red wine
- ½ teaspoon salt, plus more as needed
- ½ teaspoon pure maple syrup
- 1 cup cooked lentils (prepared from ½ cup dry)

Directions:

1. Add the celery, carrot, onion, and garlic to a food processor and process until everything is finely chopped.
2. In a Dutch oven, heat the olive oil over medium-high heat. Add the chopped mixture and sauté for about 10 minutes, stirring occasionally, or until the vegetables are lightly browned.
3. Stir in the tomatoes, wine, salt, and maple syrup and bring to a boil.
4. Once the sauce starts to boil, cover, and reduce the heat to medium-low. Simmer for 30 minutes, stirring occasionally, or until the vegetables are softened.
5. Stir in the cooked lentils and cook for an additional 5 minutes until warmed through.
6. Taste and add additional salt, if needed. Serve warm.

Nutrition Info:

- Info Per Serving: Calories: 367;Fat: 15.0g;Protein: 13.7g;Carbs: 44.5g.

Sautéed Cabbage With Parsley

Servings:4
Cooking Time: 12 To 14 Minutes
Ingredients:

- 1 small head green cabbage, cored and sliced thin
- 2 tablespoons extra-virgin olive oil, divided
- 1 onion, halved and sliced thin
- ¾ teaspoon salt, divided
- ¼ teaspoon black pepper
- ¼ cup chopped fresh parsley
- 1½ teaspoons lemon juice

Directions:
1. Place the cabbage in a large bowl with cold water. Let sit for 3 minutes. Drain well.
2. Heat 1 tablespoon of the oil in a skillet over medium-high heat until shimmering. Add the onion and ¼ teaspoon of the salt and cook for 5 to 7 minutes, or until softened and lightly browned. Transfer to a bowl.
3. Heat the remaining 1 tablespoon of the oil in now-empty skillet over medium-high heat until shimmering. Add the cabbage and sprinkle with the remaining ½ teaspoon of the salt and black pepper. Cover and cook for about 3 minutes, without stirring, or until cabbage is wilted and lightly browned on bottom.
4. Stir and continue to cook for about 4 minutes, uncovered, or until the cabbage is crisp-tender and lightly browned in places, stirring once halfway through cooking. Off heat, stir in the cooked onion, parsley and lemon juice.
5. Transfer to a plate and serve.

Nutrition Info:

- Info Per Serving: Calories: 117;Fat: 7.0g;Protein: 2.7g;Carbs: 13.4g.

Grilled Za´atar Zucchini Rounds

Servings:4
Cooking Time:20 Minutes
Ingredients:

- 2 tbsp olive oil
- 4 zucchinis, sliced
- 1 tbsp za'atar seasoning
- Salt to taste
- 2 tbsp parsley, chopped

Directions:
1. Preheat the grill on high. Cut the zucchini lengthways into ½-inch thin pieces. Brush the zucchini 'steaks' with olive oil and season with salt and za'atar seasoning. Grill for 6 minutes on both sides. Sprinkle with parsley and serve.

Nutrition Info:

- Info Per Serving: Calories: 91;Fat: 7.4g;Protein: 2.4g;Carbs: 6.6g.

Celery And Mustard Greens

Servings:4
Cooking Time: 15 Minutes
Ingredients:

- ½ cup low-sodium vegetable broth
- 1 celery stalk, roughly chopped
- ½ sweet onion, chopped
- ½ large red bell pepper, thinly sliced
- 2 garlic cloves, minced
- 1 bunch mustard greens, roughly chopped

Directions:
1. Pour the vegetable broth into a large cast iron pan and bring it to a simmer over medium heat.
2. Stir in the celery, onion, bell pepper, and garlic. Cook uncovered for about 3 to 5 minutes, or until the onion is softened.
3. Add the mustard greens to the pan and stir well. Cover, reduce the heat to low, and cook for an additional 10 minutes, or until the liquid is evaporated and the greens are wilted.
4. Remove from the heat and serve warm.

Nutrition Info:

- Info Per Serving: Calories: 39;Fat: 0g;Protein: 3.1g;Carbs: 6.8g.

Sweet Potato Chickpea Buddha Bowl

Servings:2
Cooking Time: 10 To 15 Minutes
Ingredients:
- Sauce:
- 1 tablespoon tahini
- 2 tablespoons plain Greek yogurt
- 2 tablespoons hemp seeds
- 1 garlic clove, minced
- Pinch salt
- Freshly ground black pepper, to taste
- Bowl:
- 1 small sweet potato, peeled and finely diced
- 1 teaspoon extra-virgin olive oil
- 1 cup from 1 can low-sodium chickpeas, drained and rinsed
- 2 cups baby kale

Directions:
1. Make the Sauce
2. Whisk together the tahini and yogurt in a small bowl.
3. Stir in the hemp seeds and minced garlic. Season with salt pepper. Add 2 to 3 tablespoons water to create a creamy yet pourable consistency and set aside.
4. Make the Bowl
5. Preheat the oven to 425°F. Line a baking sheet with parchment paper.
6. Place the sweet potato on the prepared baking sheet and drizzle with the olive oil. Toss well
7. Roast in the preheated oven for 10 to 15 minutes, stirring once during cooking, or until fork-tender and browned.
8. In each of 2 bowls, place ½ cup of chickpeas, 1 cup of baby kale, and half of the cooked sweet potato. Serve drizzled with half of the prepared sauce.

Nutrition Info:
- Info Per Serving: Calories: 323;Fat: 14.1g;Protein: 17.0g;Carbs: 36.0g.

Cauliflower Rice Risotto With Mushrooms

Servings:4
Cooking Time: 10 Minutes
Ingredients:
- 1 teaspoon extra-virgin olive oil
- ½ cup chopped portobello mushrooms
- 4 cups cauliflower rice
- ½ cup half-and-half
- ¼ cup low-sodium vegetable broth
- 1 cup shredded Parmesan cheese

Directions:
1. In a medium skillet, heat the olive oil over medium-low heat until shimmering.
2. Add the mushrooms and stir-fry for 3 minutes.
3. Stir in the cauliflower rice, half-and-half, and vegetable broth. Cover and bring to a boil over high heat for 5 minutes, stirring occasionally.
4. Add the Parmesan cheese and stir to combine. Continue cooking for an additional 3 minutes until the cheese is melted.
5. Divide the mixture into four bowls and serve warm.

Nutrition Info:
- Info Per Serving: Calories: 167;Fat: 10.7g;Protein: 12.1g;Carbs: 8.1g.

Grilled Eggplant "steaks" With Sauce

Servings:6
Cooking Time:20 Minutes
Ingredients:

- 2 lb eggplants, sliced lengthways
- 6 tbsp olive oil
- 5 garlic cloves, minced
- 1 tsp dried oregano
- ½ tsp red pepper flakes
- ½ cup Greek yogurt
- 3 tbsp chopped fresh parsley
- 1 tsp grated lemon zest
- 2 tsp lemon juice
- 1 tsp ground cumin
- Salt and black pepper to taste

Directions:

1. In a bowl, whisk half of the olive oil, yogurt, parsley, lemon zest and juice, cumin, and salt; set aside until ready to serve. Preheat your grill to High. Rub the eggplant steaks with the remaining olive oil, oregano, salt, and pepper. Grill them for 4-6 minutes per side until browned and tender; transfer to a serving platter. Drizzle yogurt sauce over eggplant.

Nutrition Info:

- Info Per Serving: Calories: 112;Fat: 7g;Protein: 2.6g;Carbs: 11.3g.

Veggie-stuffed Portabello Mushrooms

Servings:6
Cooking Time: 24 To 25 Minutes
Ingredients:

- 3 tablespoons extra-virgin olive oil, divided
- 1 cup diced onion
- 2 garlic cloves, minced
- 1 large zucchini, diced
- 3 cups chopped mushrooms
- 1 cup chopped tomato
- 1 teaspoon dried oregano
- ¼ teaspoon kosher salt
- ¼ teaspoon crushed red pepper
- 6 large portabello mushrooms, stems and gills removed
- Cooking spray
- 4 ounces fresh Mozzarella cheese, shredded

Directions:

1. In a large skillet over medium heat, heat 2 tablespoons of the oil. Add the onion and sauté for 4 minutes. Stir in the garlic and sauté for 1 minute.
2. Stir in the zucchini, mushrooms, tomato, oregano, salt and red pepper. Cook for 10 minutes, stirring constantly. Remove from the heat.
3. Meanwhile, heat a grill pan over medium-high heat.
4. Brush the remaining 1 tablespoon of the oil over the portabello mushroom caps. Place the mushrooms, bottom-side down, on the grill pan. Cover with a sheet of aluminum foil sprayed with nonstick cooking spray. Cook for 5 minutes.
5. Flip the mushroom caps over, and spoon about ½ cup of the cooked vegetable mixture into each cap. Top each with about 2½ tablespoons of the Mozzarella.
6. Cover and grill for 4 to 5 minutes, or until the cheese is melted.
7. Using a spatula, transfer the portabello mushrooms to a plate. Let cool for about 5 minutes before serving.

Nutrition Info:

- Info Per Serving: Calories: 111;Fat: 4.0g;Protein: 11.0g;Carbs: 11.0g.

Parsley & Olive Zucchini Bake

Servings:6
Cooking Time:1 Hour 40 Minutes
Ingredients:

- 3 tbsp olive oil
- 1 can tomatoes, diced
- 2 lb zucchinis, sliced
- 1 onion, chopped
- Salt and black pepper to taste
- 3 garlic cloves, minced
- ¼ tsp dried oregano
- ¼ tsp red pepper flakes
- 10 Kalamata olives, chopped
- 2 tbsp fresh parsley, chopped

Directions:

1. Preheat oven to 325ºF. Warm the olive oil in a saucepan over medium heat. Sauté zucchini for about 3 minutes per side; transfer to a bowl. Stir-fry the onion and salt in the same saucepan for 3-5 minutes, stirring occasionally until onion soft and lightly golden. Stir in garlic, oregano, and pepper flakes and cook until fragrant, about 30 seconds.
2. Add in olives, tomatoes, salt, and pepper, bring to a simmer, and cook for about 10 minutes, stirring occasionally. Return the zucchini, cover, and transfer the pot to the oven. Bake for 10-15 minutes. Sprinkle with parsley and serve.

Nutrition Info:

- Info Per Serving: Calories: 164;Fat: 6g;Protein: 1.5g;Carbs: 7.7g.

Balsamic Cherry Tomatoes

Servings:4
Cooking Time:10 Minutes
Ingredients:

- 2 tbsp olive oil
- 2 lb cherry tomatoes, halved
- 2 tbsp balsamic glaze
- Salt and black pepper to taste
- 1 garlic clove, minced
- 2 tbsp fresh basil, torn

Directions:

1. Warm the olive oil in a skillet over medium heat. Add the cherry tomatoes and cook for 1-2 minutes, stirring occasionally. Stir in garlic, salt, and pepper and cook until fragrant, about 30 seconds. Drizzle with balsamic glaze and decorate with basil. Serve and enjoy!

Nutrition Info:

- Info Per Serving: Calories: 45;Fat: 2.5g;Protein: 1.1g;Carbs: 5.6g.

Baked Honey Acorn Squash

Servings:4
Cooking Time:35 Minutes
Ingredients:

- 1 acorn squash, cut into wedges
- 2 tbsp olive oil
- 2 tbsp honey
- 2 tbsp rosemary, chopped
- 2 tbsp walnuts, chopped

Directions:

1. Preheat oven to 400°F. In a bowl, mix honey, rosemary, and olive oil. Lay the squash wedges on a baking sheet and drizzle with the honey mixture. Bake for 30 minutes until squash is tender and slightly caramelized, turning each slice over halfway through. Serve cooled sprinkled with walnuts.

Nutrition Info:

- Info Per Serving: Calories: 136;Fat: 6g;Protein: 0.9g;Carbs: 20g.

Garlicky Zucchini Cubes With Mint

Servings:4
Cooking Time: 10 Minutes
Ingredients:

- 3 large green zucchinis, cut into ½-inch cubes
- 3 tablespoons extra-virgin olive oil
- 1 large onion, chopped
- 3 cloves garlic, minced
- 1 teaspoon salt
- 1 teaspoon dried mint

Directions:

1. Heat the olive oil in a large skillet over medium heat.
2. Add the onion and garlic and sauté for 3 minutes, stirring constantly, or until softened.
3. Stir in the zucchini cubes and salt and cook for 5 minutes, or until the zucchini is browned and tender.
4. Add the mint to the skillet and toss to combine, then continue cooking for 2 minutes.
5. Serve warm.

Nutrition Info:

- Info Per Serving: Calories: 146;Fat: 10.6g;Protein: 4.2g;Carbs: 11.8g.

Wilted Dandelion Greens With Sweet Onion

Servings:4
Cooking Time: 15 Minutes
Ingredients:

- 1 tablespoon extra-virgin olive oil
- 2 garlic cloves, minced
- 1 Vidalia onion, thinly sliced
- ½ cup low-sodium vegetable broth
- 2 bunches dandelion greens, roughly chopped
- Freshly ground black pepper, to taste

Directions:

1. Heat the olive oil in a large skillet over low heat.
2. Add the garlic and onion and cook for 2 to 3 minutes, stirring occasionally, or until the onion is translucent.
3. Fold in the vegetable broth and dandelion greens and cook for 5 to 7 minutes until wilted, stirring frequently.
4. Sprinkle with the black pepper and serve on a plate while warm.

Nutrition Info:

- Info Per Serving: Calories: 81;Fat: 3.9g;Protein: 3.2g;Carbs: 10.8g.

Tasty Lentil Burgers

Servings:4
Cooking Time:25 Minutes
Ingredients:

- 1 cup cremini mushrooms, finely chopped
- 1 cup cooked green lentils
- ½ cup Greek yogurt
- ½ lemon, zested and juiced
- ½ tsp garlic powder
- ½ tsp dried oregano
- 1 tbsp fresh cilantro, chopped
- Salt to taste
- 3 tbsp extra-virgin olive oil
- ¼ tsp tbsp white miso
- ¼ tsp smoked paprika
- ¼ cup flour

Directions:

1. Pour ½ cup of lentils in your blender and puree partially until somewhat smooth, but with many whole lentils still remaining. In a small bowl, mix the yogurt, lemon zest and juice, garlic powder, oregano, cilantro, and salt. Season and set aside. In a medium bowl, mix the mushrooms, 2 tablespoons of olive oil, miso, and paprika. Stir in all the lentils. Add in flour and stir until the mixture everything is well incorporated. Shape the mixture into patties about ¾-inch thick. Warm the remaining olive oil in a skillet over medium heat. Fry the patties until browned and crisp, about 3 minutes. Turn and fry on the second side. Serve with the reserved yogurt mixture.

Nutrition Info:

- Info Per Serving: Calories: 215;Fat: 13g;Protein: 10g;Carbs: 19g.

Baked Vegetable Stew

Servings:6
Cooking Time:70 Minutes
Ingredients:
- 1 can diced tomatoes, drained with juice reserved
- 3 tbsp olive oil
- 1 onion, chopped
- 2 tbsp fresh oregano, minced
- 1 tsp paprika
- 4 garlic cloves, minced
- 1 ½ lb green beans, sliced
- 1 lb Yukon Gold potatoes, peeled and chopped
- 1 tbsp tomato paste
- Salt and black pepper to taste
- 3 tbsp fresh basil, chopped

Directions:
1. Preheat oven to 360°F. Warm the olive oil in a skillet over medium heat. Sauté onion and garlic for 3 minutes until softened. Stir in oregano and paprika for 30 seconds. Transfer to a baking dish and add in green beans, potatoes, tomatoes, tomato paste, salt, pepper, and 1 ½ cups of water; stir well. Bake for 40-50 minutes. Sprinkle with basil. Serve.

Nutrition Info:
- Info Per Serving: Calories: 121;Fat: 0.8g;Protein: 4.2g;Carbs: 26g.

Roasted Vegetables And Chickpeas

Servings:2
Cooking Time: 30 Minutes
Ingredients:
- 4 cups cauliflower florets (about ½ small head)
- 2 medium carrots, peeled, halved, and then sliced into quarters lengthwise
- 2 tablespoons olive oil, divided
- ½ teaspoon garlic powder, divided
- ½ teaspoon salt, divided
- 2 teaspoons za'atar spice mix, divided
- 1 can chickpeas, drained, rinsed, and patted dry
- ¾ cup plain Greek yogurt
- 1 teaspoon harissa spice paste

Directions:
1. Preheat the oven to 400ºF. Line a sheet pan with foil or parchment paper.
2. Place the cauliflower and carrots in a large bowl. Drizzle with 1 tablespoon olive oil and sprinkle with ¼ teaspoon of garlic powder, ¼ teaspoon of salt, and 1 teaspoon of za'atar. Toss well to combine.
3. Spread the vegetables onto one half of the sheet pan in a single layer.
4. Place the chickpeas in the same bowl and season with the remaining 1 tablespoon of oil, ¼ teaspoon of garlic powder, and ¼ teaspoon of salt, and the remaining za'atar. Toss well to combine.
5. Spread the chickpeas onto the other half of the sheet pan.
6. Roast for 30 minutes, or until the vegetables are tender and the chickpeas start to turn golden. Flip the vegetables halfway through the cooking time, and give the chickpeas a stir so they cook evenly.
7. The chickpeas may need an extra few minutes if you like them crispy. If so, remove the vegetables and leave the chickpeas in until they're cooked to desired crispiness.
8. Meanwhile, combine the yogurt and harissa in a small bowl. Taste and add additional harissa as desired, then serve.

Nutrition Info:
- Info Per Serving: Calories: 468;Fat: 23.0g;Protein: 18.1g;Carbs: 54.1g.

Minty Broccoli & Walnuts

Servings:2
Cooking Time:10 Minutes
Ingredients:
- 1 garlic clove, minced
- ½ cups walnuts, chopped
- 3 cups broccoli florets, steamed
- 1 tbsp mint, chopped
- ½ lemon, juiced
- Salt and black pepper to taste

Directions:
1. Mix walnuts, broccoli, garlic, mint, lemon juice, salt, and pepper in a bowl. Serve chilled.

Nutrition Info:
- Info Per Serving: Calories: 210;Fat: 7g;Protein: 4g;Carbs: 9g.

Buttery Garlic Green Beans

Servings:6
Cooking Time:25 Minutes
Ingredients:
- 2 tbsp butter
- 1 lb green beans, trimmed
- 4 cups water
- 6 garlic cloves, minced
- 1 shallot, chopped
- Celery salt to taste
- ½ tsp red pepper flakes

Directions:
1. Pour 4 cups of water in a pot over high heat and bring to a boil. Cut the green beans in half crosswise. Reduce the heat and add in the green beans. Simmer for 6-8 minutes until crisp-tender but still vibrant green. Drain beans and set aside.
2. Melt the butter in a pan over medium heat and sauté garlic and shallot for 3 minutes until the garlic is slightly browned and fragrant. Stir in the beans and season with celery salt. Cook for 2–3 minutes. Serve topped with red pepper flakes.

Nutrition Info:
- Info Per Serving: Calories: 65;Fat: 4g;Protein: 2g;Carbs: 7g.

Baby Kale And Cabbage Salad

Servings:6
Cooking Time: 0 Minutes
Ingredients:
- 2 bunches baby kale, thinly sliced
- ½ head green savoy cabbage, cored and thinly sliced
- 1 medium red bell pepper, thinly sliced
- 1 garlic clove, thinly sliced
- 1 cup toasted peanuts
- Dressing:
- Juice of 1 lemon
- ¼ cup apple cider vinegar
- 1 teaspoon ground cumin
- ¼ teaspoon smoked paprika

Directions:
1. In a large mixing bowl, toss together the kale and cabbage.
2. Make the dressing: Whisk together the lemon juice, vinegar, cumin and paprika in a small bowl.
3. Pour the dressing over the greens and gently massage with your hands.
4. Add the pepper, garlic and peanuts to the mixing bowl. Toss to combine.
5. Serve immediately.

Nutrition Info:
- Info Per Serving: Calories: 199;Fat: 12.0g;Protein: 10.0g;Carbs: 17.0g.

Roasted Caramelized Root Vegetables

Servings:6
Cooking Time:40 Minutes

Ingredients:

- 1 sweet potato, peeled and cut into chunks
- 3 tbsp olive oil
- 2 carrots, peeled
- 2 beets, peeled
- 1 turnip, peeled
- 1 tsp cumin
- 1 tsp sweet paprika
- Salt and black pepper to taste
- 1 lemon, juiced
- 2 tbsp parsley, chopped

Directions:

1. Preheat oven to 400ºF. Cut the vegetables into chunks and toss them with olive oil and seasonings in a sheet pan. Drizzle with lemon juice and roast them for 35-40 minutes until vegetables are tender and golden. Serve topped with parsley.

Nutrition Info:

- Info Per Serving: Calories: 80;Fat: 4.8g;Protein: 1.5g;Carbs: 8.9g.

Chili Vegetable Skillet

Servings:4
Cooking Time:30 Minutes

Ingredients:

- 1 cup condensed cream of mushroom soup
- 1 ½ lb eggplants, cut into chunks
- 1 cup cremini mushrooms, sliced
- 4 tbsp olive oil
- 1 carrot, thinly sliced
- 1 can tomatoes
- ½ cup red onion, thinly sliced
- 2 garlic cloves, minced
- 1 tsp fresh rosemary
- 1 tsp chili pepper
- Salt and black pepper to taste
- 2 tbsp parsley, chopped
- ¼ cup Parmesan cheese, grated

Directions:

1. Warm the olive oil in a skillet over medium heat. Add in the eggplant and cook until golden brown on all sides, about 5 minutes; set aside. Add in the carrot, onion, and mushrooms and sauté for 4 more minutes to the same skillet. Add in garlic, rosemary, and chili pepper. Cook for another 30-40 seconds. Add in 1 cup of water, cream of mushroom soup, and tomatoes. Bring to a boil and lower the heat; simmer covered for 5 minutes. Mix in sautéed eggplants and parsley and cook for 10 more minutes. Sprinkle with salt and black pepper. Serve topped with Parmesan cheese.

Nutrition Info:

- Info Per Serving: Calories: 261;Fat: 18.7g;Protein: 5g;Carbs: 23g.

Spicy Potato Wedges

Servings:4
Cooking Time:30 Minutes

Ingredients:

- 1 ½ lb potatoes, peeled and cut into wedges
- 3 tbsp olive oil
- 1 tbsp minced fresh rosemary
- 2 tsp chili powder
- 3 garlic cloves, minced
- Salt and black pepper to taste

Directions:

1. Preheat the oven to 370ºF. Toss the wedges with olive oil, garlic, salt, and pepper. Spread out in a roasting sheet. Roast for 15-20 minutes until browned and crisp at the edges. Remove and sprinkle with chili powder and rosemary.

Nutrition Info:

- Info Per Serving: Calories: 152;Fat: 7g;Protein: 2.5g;Carbs: 21g.

Mushroom & Cauliflower Roast

Servings:4
Cooking Time:35 Minutes
Ingredients:

- 2 tbsp olive oil
- 4 cups cauliflower florets
- 1 celery stalk, chopped
- 1 cup mushrooms, sliced
- 10 cherry tomatoes, halved
- 1 yellow onion, chopped
- 2 garlic cloves, minced
- 2 tbsp dill, chopped
- Salt and black pepper to taste

Directions:

1. Preheat the oven to 340ºF. Line a baking sheet with parchment paper. Place in cauliflower florets, olive oil, mushrooms, celery, tomatoes, onion, garlic, salt, and pepper and mix to combine. Bake for 25 minutes. Serve topped with dill.

Nutrition Info:

- Info Per Serving: Calories: 380;Fat: 15g;Protein: 12g;Carbs: 17g.

Mini Crustless Spinach Quiches

Servings:6
Cooking Time: 20 Minutes
Ingredients:

- 2 tablespoons extra-virgin olive oil
- 1 onion, finely chopped
- 2 cups baby spinach
- 2 garlic cloves, minced
- 8 large eggs, beaten
- ¼ cup unsweetened almond milk
- ½ teaspoon sea salt
- ¼ teaspoon freshly ground black pepper
- 1 cup shredded Swiss cheese
- Cooking spray

Directions:

1. Preheat the oven to 375ºF. Spritz a 6-cup muffin tin with cooking spray. Set aside.
2. In a large skillet over medium-high heat, heat the olive oil until shimmering. Add the onion and cook for about 4 minutes, or until soft. Add the spinach and cook for about 1 minute, stirring constantly, or until the spinach softens. Add the garlic and sauté for 30 seconds. Remove from the heat and let cool.
3. In a medium bowl, whisk together the eggs, milk, salt and pepper.
4. Stir the cooled vegetables and the cheese into the egg mixture. Spoon the mixture into the prepared muffin tins. Bake for about 15 minutes, or until the eggs are set.
5. Let rest for 5 minutes before serving.

Nutrition Info:

- Info Per Serving: Calories: 218;Fat: 17.0g;Protein: 14.0g;Carbs: 4.0g.

Beans , Grains, And Pastas Recipes

Sardine & Caper Tagliatelle

Servings:4
Cooking Time:20 Minutes
Ingredients:

- 1 tbsp olive oil
- 8 oz tagliatelle
- ¼ cup chopped onion
- 2 garlic cloves, minced
- 1 tsp tomato paste
- 16 canned sardines in olive oil
- 1 tbsp capers
- ½ cup grated Parmesan cheese
- Salt and black pepper to taste
- 1 tbsp chopped parsley
- 1 tsp chopped oregano

Directions:
1. Boil water in a pot over medium heat and place in the pasta. Cook for 8-10 minutes for al dente. Drain and set aside; reserve ½ cup of the cooking liquid. Warm the olive oil in a pan over medium heat. Place in onion, garlic, and oregano and cook for 5 minutes until soft. Stir in salt, tomato paste, pepper, and ½ cup of reserved liquid for 1 minute. Mix in cooked pasta, capers, and sardines and toss to coat. Serve topped with Parmesan cheese and parsley.

Nutrition Info:
- Info Per Serving: Calories: 412;Fat: 13g;Protein: 23g;Carbs: 47g.

Rich Cauliflower Alfredo

Servings:4
Cooking Time: 30 Minutes
Ingredients:

- Cauliflower Alfredo Sauce:
- 1 tablespoon avocado oil
- ½ yellow onion, diced
- 2 cups cauliflower florets
- 2 garlic cloves, minced
- 1½ teaspoons miso
- 1 teaspoon Dijon mustard
- Pinch of ground nutmeg
- ½ cup unsweetened almond milk
- 1½ tablespoons fresh lemon juice
- 2 tablespoons nutritional yeast
- Sea salt and ground black pepper, to taste
- Fettuccine:
- 1 tablespoon avocado oil
- ½ yellow onion, diced
- 1 cup broccoli florets
- 1 zucchini, halved lengthwise and cut into ¼-inch-thick half-moons
- Sea salt and ground black pepper, to taste
- ½ cup sun-dried tomatoes, drained if packed in oil
- 8 ounces cooked whole-wheat fettuccine
- ½ cup fresh basil, cut into ribbons

Directions:
1. Make the Sauce:
2. Heat the avocado oil in a nonstick skillet over medium-high heat until shimmering.
3. Add half of the onion to the skillet and sauté for 5 minutes or until translucent.
4. Add the cauliflower and garlic to the skillet. Reduce the heat to low and cook for 8 minutes or until the cauliflower is tender.
5. Pour them in a food processor, add the remaining ingredients for the sauce and pulse to combine well. Set aside.
6. Make the Fettuccine:
7. Heat the avocado oil in a nonstick skillet over medium-high heat.
8. Add the remaining half of onion and sauté for 5 minutes or until translucent.
9. Add the broccoli and zucchini. Sprinkle with salt and ground black pepper, then sauté for 5 minutes or until tender.
10. Add the sun-dried tomatoes, reserved sauce, and fettuccine. Sauté for 3 minutes or until well-coated and heated through.
11. Serve the fettuccine on a large plate and spread with basil before serving.

Nutrition Info:
- Info Per Serving: Calories: 288;Fat: 15.9g;Protein: 10.1g;Carbs: 32.5g.

Rigatoni With Peppers & Mozzarella

Servings:4
Cooking Time:30 Min + Marinating Time
Ingredients:
- 1 lb fresh mozzarella cheese, cubed
- 3 tbsp olive oil
- ¼ cup chopped fresh chives
- ¼ cup basil, chopped
- ½ tsp red pepper flakes
- 1 tsp apple cider vinegar
- Salt and black pepper to taste
- 3 garlic cloves, minced
- 2 cups sliced onions
- 3 cups bell peppers, sliced
- 2 cups tomato sauce
- 8 oz rigatoni
- 1 tbsp butter
- ¼ cup grated Parmesan cheese

Directions:
1. Bring to a boil salted water in a pot over high heat. Add the rigatoni and cook according to package directions. Drain and set aside, reserving 1 cup of the cooking water. Combine the mozzarella, 1 tablespoon of olive oil, chives, basil, pepper flakes, apple cider vinegar, salt, and pepper. Let the cheese marinate for 30 minutes at room temperature.
2. Warm the remaining olive oil in a large skillet over medium heat. Stir-fry the garlic for 10 seconds and add the onions and peppers. Cook for 3-4 minutes, stirring occasionally until the onions are translucent. Pour in the tomato sauce, and reduce the heat to a simmer. Add the rigatoni and reserved cooking water and toss to coat. Heat off and adjust the seasoning with salt and pepper. Toss with marinated mozzarella cheese and butter. Sprinkle with Parmesan cheese and serve.

Nutrition Info:
- Info Per Serving: Calories: 434;Fat: 18g;Protein: 44g;Carbs: 27g.

Caprese Pasta With Roasted Asparagus

Servings:6
Cooking Time: 25 Minutes
Ingredients:
- 8 ounces uncooked small pasta, like orecchiette (little ears) or farfalle (bow ties)
- 1½ pounds fresh asparagus, ends trimmed and stalks chopped into 1-inch pieces
- 1½ cups grape tomatoes, halved
- 2 tablespoons extra-virgin olive oil
- ¼ teaspoon kosher salt
- ¼ teaspoon freshly ground black pepper
- 2 cups fresh Mozzarella, drained and cut into bite-size pieces
- ⅓ cup torn fresh basil leaves
- 2 tablespoons balsamic vinegar

Directions:
1. Preheat the oven to 400°F.
2. In a large stockpot of salted water, cook the pasta for about 8 to 10 minutes. Drain and reserve about ¼ cup of the cooking liquid.
3. Meanwhile, in a large bowl, toss together the asparagus, tomatoes, oil, salt and pepper. Spread the mixture onto a large, rimmed baking sheet and bake in the oven for 15 minutes, stirring twice during cooking.
4. Remove the vegetables from the oven and add the cooked pasta to the baking sheet. Mix with a few tablespoons of cooking liquid to help the sauce become smoother and the saucy vegetables stick to the pasta.
5. Gently mix in the Mozzarella and basil. Drizzle with the balsamic vinegar. Serve from the baking sheet or pour the pasta into a large bowl.

Nutrition Info:
- Info Per Serving: Calories: 147;Fat: 3.0g;Protein: 16.0g;Carbs: 17.0g.

Basic Brown Rice Pilaf With Capers

Servings:4
Cooking Time:30 Minutes
Ingredients:

- 2 tbsp olive oil
- 1 cup brown rice
- 1 onion, chopped
- 1 celery stalk, chopped
- 2 garlic cloves, minced
- ½ cup capers, rinsed
- Salt and black pepper to taste
- 2 tbsp parsley, chopped

Directions:

1. Warm the olive oil in a skillet over medium heat. Sauté celery, garlic, and onion for 10 minutes. Stir in rice, capers, 2 cups of water, salt, and pepper and cook for 25 minutes. Serve topped with parsley.

Nutrition Info:

- Info Per Serving: Calories: 230;Fat: 8.9g;Protein: 7g;Carbs: 16g.

Mozzarella & Asparagus Pasta

Servings:6
Cooking Time:40 Minutes
Ingredients:

- 1 ½ lb asparagus, trimmed, cut into 1-inch
- 2 tbsp olive oil
- 8 oz orecchiette
- 2 cups cherry tomatoes, halved
- Salt and black pepper to taste
- 2 cups fresh mozzarella, drained and chopped
- ⅓ cup torn basil leaves
- 2 tbsp balsamic vinegar

Directions:

1. Preheat oven to 390° F. In a large pot, cook the pasta according to the directions. Drain, reserving ¼ cup of cooking water.
2. In the meantime, in a large bowl, toss in asparagus, cherry tomatoes, oil, pepper, and salt. Spread the mixture onto a rimmed baking sheet and bake for 15 minutes, stirring twice throughout cooking. Remove the veggies from the oven, and add the cooked pasta to the baking sheet. Mix with a few tbsp of pasta water to smooth the sauce and veggies. Slowly mix in the mozzarella and basil. Drizzle with the balsamic vinegar and serve in bowls.

Nutrition Info:

- Info Per Serving: Calories: 188;Fat: 11g;Protein: 14g;Carbs: 23g.

Chickpea Salad With Tomatoes And Basil

Servings:2
Cooking Time: 45 Minutes
Ingredients:

- 1 cup dried chickpeas, rinsed
- 1 quart water, or enough to cover the chickpeas by 3 to 4 inches
- 1½ cups halved grape tomatoes
- 1 cup chopped fresh basil leaves
- 2 to 3 tablespoons balsamic vinegar
- ½ teaspoon garlic powder
- ½ teaspoon salt, plus more as needed

Directions:

1. In your Instant Pot, combine the chickpeas and water.
2. Secure the lid. Select the Manual mode and set the cooking time for 45 minutes at High Pressure.
3. Once cooking is complete, do a natural pressure release for 20 minutes, then release any remaining pressure. Carefully open the lid and drain the chickpeas. Refrigerate to cool (unless you want to serve this warm, which is good, too).
4. While the chickpeas cool, in a large bowl, stir together the basil, tomatoes, vinegar, garlic powder, and salt. Add the beans, stir to combine, and serve.

Nutrition Info:

- Info Per Serving: Calories: 395;Fat: 6.0g;Protein: 19.8g;Carbs: 67.1g.

Old-fashioned Pasta Primavera

Servings:4
Cooking Time:25 Minutes
Ingredients:

- ½ cup grated Pecorino Romano cheese
- 2 cups cauliflower florets, cut into matchsticks
- ¼ cup olive oil
- 16 oz tortiglioni
- ½ cup chopped green onions
- 1 red bell pepper, sliced
- 4 garlic cloves, minced
- 1 cup grape tomatoes, halved
- 2 tsp dried Italian seasoning
- ½ lemon, juiced

Directions:

1. In a pot of boiling water, cook the tortiglioni pasta for 8-10 minutes until al dente. Drain and set aside.
2. Heat olive oil in a skillet and sauté onion, cauliflower, and bell pepper for 7 minutes. Mix in garlic and cook until fragrant, 30 seconds. Stir in the tomatoes and Italian seasoning; cook until the tomatoes soften, 5 minutes. Mix in the lemon juice and tortiglioni. Garnish with cheese.

Nutrition Info:

- Info Per Serving: Calories: 283;Fat: 18g;Protein: 15g;Carbs: 5g.

Citrusy & Minty Farro

Servings:6
Cooking Time:28 Minutes
Ingredients:

- 3 tbsp olive oil
- 1 ½ cups whole farro
- Salt and black pepper to taste
- 1 onion, chopped fine
- 1 garlic clove, minced
- ¼ cup chopped fresh cilantro
- ¼ cup chopped fresh mint
- 1 tbsp lemon juice

Directions:

1. Bring 4 quarts of water to boil in a pot. Add farro and season with salt and pepper, bring to a boil and cook until grains are tender with a slight chew, 20-25 minutes. Drain farro, return to the empty pot and cover to keep warm. Heat 2 tbsp of oil in a large skillet over medium heat. Stir-fry onion for 5 minutes. Stir in garlic and cook until fragrant, about 30 seconds. Add the remaining oil and farro and stir-fry for 2 minutes. Remove from heat, stir in cilantro, mint, and lemon juice. Season to taste and serve.

Nutrition Info:

- Info Per Serving: Calories: 322;Fat: 16g;Protein: 11g;Carbs: 24g.

Authentic Fava Bean & Garbanzo Fül

Servings:6
Cooking Time:20 Minutes
Ingredients:

- 3 tbsp extra-virgin olive oil
- 1 can garbanzo beans
- 1 can fava beans
- ½ tsp lemon zest
- ½ tsp dried oregano
- ½ cup lemon juice
- 3 cloves garlic, minced
- Salt to taste

Directions:

1. Place the garbanzo beans, fava beans, and 3 cups of water in a pot over medium heat. Cook for 10 minutes. Drain the beans Reserving 1 cup of the liquid, and put them in a bowl. Mix the reserved liquid, lemon juice, lemon zest, oregano, minced garlic, and salt together and add to the beans in the bowl. With a potato masher, mash up about half the beans in the bowl. Stir the mixture to combine. Drizzle the olive oil over the top. Serve with pita bread if desired.

Nutrition Info:

- Info Per Serving: Calories: 199;Fat: 9g;Protein: 10g;Carbs: 25g.

Raspberry & Nut Quinoa

Servings:4
Cooking Time:5 Minutes
Ingredients:
- 1 tbsp honey
- 2 cups almond milk
- 2 cups quinoa, cooked
- ½ tsp cinnamon powder
- 1 cup raspberries
- ¼ cup walnuts, chopped

Directions:
1. Combine quinoa, milk, cinnamon powder, honey, raspberries, and walnuts in a bowl. Serve in individual bowls.

Nutrition Info:
- Info Per Serving: Calories: 300;Fat: 15g;Protein: 5g;Carbs: 15g.

Baked Rolled Oat With Pears And Pecans

Servings:6
Cooking Time: 30 Minutes
Ingredients:
- 2 tablespoons coconut oil, melted, plus more for greasing the pan
- 3 ripe pears, cored and diced
- 2 cups unsweetened almond milk
- 1 tablespoon pure vanilla extract
- ¼ cup pure maple syrup
- 2 cups gluten-free rolled oats
- ½ cup raisins
- ¾ cup chopped pecans
- ¼ teaspoon ground nutmeg
- 1 teaspoon ground cinnamon
- ½ teaspoon ground ginger
- ¼ teaspoon sea salt

Directions:
1. Preheat the oven to 350ºF. Grease a baking dish with melted coconut oil, then spread the pears in a single layer on the baking dish evenly.
2. Combine the almond milk, vanilla extract, maple syrup, and coconut oil in a bowl. Stir to mix well.
3. Combine the remaining ingredients in a separate large bowl. Stir to mix well. Fold the almond milk mixture in the bowl, then pour the mixture over the pears.
4. Place the baking dish in the preheated oven and bake for 30 minutes or until lightly browned and set.
5. Serve immediately.

Nutrition Info:
- Info Per Serving: Calories: 479;Fat: 34.9g;Protein: 8.8g;Carbs: 50.1g.

Simple Lentil Risotto

Servings:2
Cooking Time: 20 Minutes
Ingredients:

- ½ tablespoon olive oil
- ½ medium onion, chopped
- ½ cup dry lentils, soaked overnight
- ½ celery stalk, chopped
- 1 sprig parsley, chopped
- ½ cup Arborio (short-grain Italian) rice
- 1 garlic clove, lightly mashed
- 2 cups vegetable stock

Directions:

1. Press the Sauté button to heat your Instant Pot.
2. Add the oil and onion to the Instant Pot and sauté for 5 minutes.
3. Add all the remaining ingredients to the Instant Pot.
4. Secure the lid. Select the Manual mode and set the cooking time for 15 minutes at High Pressure.
5. Once cooking is complete, do a natural pressure release for 20 minutes, then release any remaining pressure. Carefully open the lid.
6. Stir and serve hot.

Nutrition Info:

- Info Per Serving: Calories: 261;Fat: 3.6g;Protein: 10.6g;Carbs: 47.1g.

Hot Zucchini Millet

Servings:4
Cooking Time:30 Minutes
Ingredients:

- 3 tbsp olive oil
- 2 tomatoes, chopped
- 2 zucchinis, chopped
- 1 cup millet
- 2 spring onions, chopped
- ½ cup cilantro, chopped
- 1 tsp chili paste
- ½ cup lemon juice
- Salt and black pepper to taste

Directions:

1. Warm the olive oil in a skillet over medium heat and sauté millet for 1-2 minutes. Pour in 2 cups of water, salt, and pepper and bring to a simmer. Cook for 15 minutes. Mix in spring onions, tomatoes, zucchini, chili paste, and lemon juice. Serve topped with cilantro.

Nutrition Info:

- Info Per Serving: Calories: 230;Fat: 11g;Protein: 3g;Carbs: 15g.

Spicy Chicken Lentils

Servings:4
Cooking Time:1 Hour 20 Minutes
Ingredients:

- 2 tbsp olive oil
- 1 lb chicken thighs, skinless, boneless, and cubed
- 1 tbsp coriander seeds
- 1 bay leaf
- 1 tbsp tomato paste
- 2 carrots, chopped
- 1 onion, chopped
- 2 garlic cloves, chopped
- ½ tsp red chili flakes
- ½ tsp paprika
- 4 cups chicken stock
- 1 cup brown lentils
- Salt and black pepper to taste

Directions:

1. Warm the olive oil in a pot over medium heat and cook chicken, onion, and garlic for 6-8 minutes. Stir in carrots, tomato paste, coriander seeds, bay leaf, red chili pepper, and paprika for 3 minutes. Pour in the chicken stock and bring to a boil. Simmer for 25 minutes. Add in lentils, season with salt and pepper and cook for another 15 minutes. Discard bay leaf and serve right away.

Nutrition Info:

- Info Per Serving: Calories: 320;Fat: 14g;Protein: 14g;Carbs: 18g.

Fava And Garbanzo Bean Ful

Servings:6
Cooking Time: 10 Minutes
Ingredients:

- 1 can fava beans, rinsed and drained
- 1 can garbanzo beans, rinsed and drained
- 3 cups water
- ½ cup lemon juice
- 3 cloves garlic, peeled and minced
- 1 teaspoon salt
- 3 tablespoons extra-virgin olive oil

Directions:

1. In a pot over medium heat, cook the beans and water for 10 minutes.
2. Drain the beans and transfer to a bowl. Reserve 1 cup of the liquid from the cooked beans.
3. Add the reserved liquid, lemon juice, minced garlic and salt to the bowl with the beans. Mix to combine well. Using a potato masher, mash up about half the beans in the bowl.
4. Give the mixture one more stir to make sure the beans are evenly mixed.
5. Drizzle with the olive oil and serve.

Nutrition Info:

- Info Per Serving: Calories: 199;Fat: 9.0g;Protein: 10.0g;Carbs: 25.0g.

Wild Rice With Cheese & Mushrooms

Servings:4
Cooking Time:30 Minutes
Ingredients:

- 2 cups chicken stock
- 1 cup wild rice
- 1 onion, chopped
- ½ lb wild mushrooms, sliced
- 2 garlic cloves, minced
- 1 lemon, juiced and zested
- 1 tbsp chives, chopped
- ½ cup mozzarella, grated
- Salt and black pepper to taste

Directions:

1. Warm chicken stock in a pot over medium heat and add in wild rice, onion, mushrooms, garlic, lemon juice, lemon zest, salt, and pepper. Bring to a simmer and cook for 20 minutes. Transfer to a baking tray and top with mozzarella cheese. Place the tray under the broiler for 4 minutes until the cheese is melted. Sprinkle with chives and serve.

Nutrition Info:

- Info Per Serving: Calories: 230;Fat: 6g;Protein: 6g;Carbs: 13g.

Milanese-style Risotto

Servings:4
Cooking Time:10 Minutes
Ingredients:

- 2 tbsp olive oil
- 2 tbsp butter, softened
- 1 cup Arborio rice, cooked
- ½ cup white wine
- 1 onion, chopped
- Salt and black pepper to taste
- 2 cups hot chicken stock
- 1 pinch of saffron, soaked
- ½ cup Parmesan, grated

Directions:

1. Warm the olive oil in a skillet over medium heat and sauté onion for 3 minutes. Stir in rice, salt, and pepper for 1 minute. Pour in white wine and saffron and stir to deglaze the bottom of the skillet. Gradually add in the chicken stock while stirring; cook for 15-18 minutes. Turn off the heat and mix in butter and Parmesan cheese. Serve immediately.

Nutrition Info:

- Info Per Serving: Calories: 250;Fat: 10g;Protein: 5g;Carbs: 18g.

One-pot Linguine With Brussels Sprouts

Servings:4
Cooking Time:35 Minutes
Ingredients:

- 8 oz whole-wheat linguine
- ⅔ cup + 2 tbsp olive oil
- 1 medium sweet onion, diced
- 2 garlic cloves, minced
- 1 tsp red chili flakes
- 1 lb Brussels sprouts, shredded
- ½ cup chicken stock
- ⅔ cup dry white wine
- ½ cup grated Parmesan cheese
- 1 lemon, juiced
- 2 tbsp parsley, chopped

Directions:

1. Cook pasta in boiling salted water according to package directions. Reserve 1 cup of the pasta water. Drain the linguine and mix with 2 tablespoons of olive oil; set aside.
2. Warm the remaining olive oil in a skillet over medium heat. Sauté the onion for 3 minutes, until softened. Add the garlic and cook for 1 minute, until fragrant. Stir in the Brussels sprouts and cook covered for 15 minutes. Pour in chicken stock and cook for 3-4 more minutes until the sprouts are fork-tender. Add white wine and cook for 5-7 minutes, until reduced. Add the pasta to the skillet and the pasta water. Serve with Parmesan cheese, chili flakes, and lemon juice.

Nutrition Info:

- Info Per Serving: Calories: 501;Fat: 31g;Protein: 15g;Carbs: 49g.

Bell Pepper & Bean Salad

Servings:6
Cooking Time:30 Minutes
Ingredients:

- ¼ cup extra-virgin olive oil
- 3 garlic cloves, minced
- 2 cans cannellini beans
- Salt and black pepper to taste
- 2 tsp sherry vinegar
- 1 red onion, sliced
- 1 red bell pepper, chopped
- ¼ cup chopped fresh parsley
- 2 tsp chopped fresh chives
- ¼ tsp crushed red pepper

Directions:

1. Warm 1 tbsp of olive oil in a saucepan over medium heat. Sauté the garlic until it turns golden but not brown, about 3 minutes. Add beans, 2 cups of water, and salt, and pepper, and bring to a simmer. Heat off. Let sit for 20 minutes.
2. Mix well the vinegar and red onion in a salad bowl. Drain the beans and remove the garlic. Add beans, remaining olive oil, bell pepper, parsley, crushed red pepper, chives, salt, and pepper to the onion mixture and gently toss to combine.

Nutrition Info:

- Info Per Serving: Calories: 131;Fat: 7.7g;Protein: 6g;Carbs: 13.5g.

Easy Walnut And Ricotta Spaghetti

Servings:6
Cooking Time: 10 Minutes
Ingredients:

- 1 pound cooked whole-wheat spaghetti
- 2 tablespoons extra-virgin olive oil
- 4 cloves garlic, minced
- ¾ cup walnuts, toasted and finely chopped
- 2 tablespoons ricotta cheese
- ¼ cup flat-leaf parsley, chopped
- ½ cup grated Parmesan cheese
- Sea salt and freshly ground pepper, to taste

Directions:

1. Reserve a cup of spaghetti water while cooking the spaghetti.
2. Heat the olive oil in a nonstick skillet over medium-low heat or until shimmering.
3. Add the garlic and sauté for a minute or until fragrant.
4. Pour the spaghetti water into the skillet and cook for 8 more minutes.
5. Turn off the heat and mix in the walnuts and ricotta cheese.
6. Put the cooked spaghetti on a large serving plate, then pour the walnut sauce over. Spread with parsley and Parmesan, then sprinkle with salt and ground pepper. Toss to serve.

Nutrition Info:

- Info Per Serving: Calories: 264;Fat: 16.8g;Protein: 8.6g;Carbs: 22.8g.

Spanish-style Linguine With Tapenade

Servings:4
Cooking Time:20 Minutes
Ingredients:

- 1 cup black olives, pitted
- 2 tbsp capers
- 2 tbsp rosemary, chopped
- 1 garlic clove, smashed
- 2 anchovy fillets, chopped
- ½ tsp sugar
- ⅔ cup + 2 tbsp olive oil
- 1 lb linguine
- ½ cup grated Manchego cheese
- 1 tbsp chopped fresh chives

Directions:

1. Process the olives, capers, rosemary, garlic, anchovies, sugar, and ⅔ cup olive oil in your food processor until well incorporated but not smooth; set aside. Bring a large pot of salted water to a boil, add the linguine, and cook for 7-9 minutes until al dente. Drain the pasta in a bowl and add the remaining 2 tablespoons olive oil and Manchego cheese; toss to coat. Arrange pasta on a serving platter and top it with tapenade and chives. Serve and enjoy!

Nutrition Info:

- Info Per Serving: Calories: 375;Fat: 39g;Protein: 5g;Carbs: 23g.

Mushroom Bulgur Pilaf With Almonds

Servings:2
Cooking Time:45 Minutes
Ingredients:

- 3 scallions, minced
- 2 oz mushrooms, sliced
- 1 tbsp olive oil
- 1 garlic clove, minced
- ¼ cup almonds, sliced
- ½ cup bulgur
- 1 ½ cups chicken stock
- ½ tsp dried thyme
- 1 tbsp parsley, chopped
- Salt to taste

Directions:

1. Warm the olive oil in a saucepan over medium heat. Add garlic, scallions, mushrooms, and almonds, and sauté for 3 minutes. Pour the bulgur and cook, stirring, for 1 minute to toast it. Add the stock and thyme and bring the mixture to a boil. Cover and reduce the heat to low. Simmer the bulgur for 25 minutes or until the liquid is absorbed and the bulgur is tender. Sprinkle with parsley and season with salt to serve.

Nutrition Info:

- Info Per Serving: Calories: 342;Fat: 15g;Protein: 11g;Carbs: 48g.

Carrot & Barley Risotto

Servings:6
Cooking Time:1 Hour 20 Minutes
Ingredients:

- 2 tbsp olive oil
- 4 cups vegetable broth
- 4 cups water
- 1 onion, chopped fine
- 1 carrot, chopped
- 1 ½ cups pearl barley
- 1 cup dry white wine
- ¼ tsp dried oregano
- 2 oz Parmesan cheese, grated
- Salt and black pepper to taste

Directions:

1. Bring broth and water to a simmer in a saucepan. Reduce heat to low and cover to keep warm.
2. Heat 1 tbsp of oil in a pot over medium heat until sizzling. Stir-fry onion and carrot until softened, 6-7 minutes. Add barley and cook, stirring often, until lightly toasted and aromatic, 4 minutes. Add wine and cook, stirring frequently for 2 minutes. Stir in 3 cups of water and oregano, bring to a simmer, and cook, stirring occasionally until liquid is absorbed, 25 minutes. Stir in 2 cups of broth, bring to a simmer, and cook until the liquid is absorbed, 15 minutes.
3. Continue cooking, stirring often and adding warm broth as needed to prevent the pot bottom from becoming dry until barley is cooked through but still somewhat firm in the center, 15-20 minutes. Off heat, adjust consistency with the remaining warm broth as needed. Stir in Parmesan and the remaining oil and season with salt and pepper to taste. Serve.

Nutrition Info:

- Info Per Serving: Calories: 355;Fat: 21g;Protein: 16g;Carbs: 35g.

Minestrone Chickpeas And Macaroni Casserole

Servings:5
Cooking Time: 7 Hours 20 Minutes
Ingredients:

- 1 can chickpeas, drained and rinsed
- 1 can diced tomatoes, with the juice
- 1 can no-salt-added tomato paste
- 3 medium carrots, sliced
- 3 cloves garlic, minced
- 1 medium yellow onion, chopped
- 1 cup low-sodium vegetable soup
- ½ teaspoon dried rosemary
- 1 teaspoon dried oregano
- 2 teaspoons maple syrup
- ½ teaspoon sea salt
- ¼ teaspoon ground black pepper
- ½ pound fresh green beans, trimmed and cut into bite-size pieces
- 1 cup macaroni pasta
- 2 ounces Parmesan cheese, grated

Directions:

1. Except for the green beans, pasta, and Parmesan cheese, combine all the ingredients in the slow cooker and stir to mix well.
2. Put the slow cooker lid on and cook on low for 7 hours.
3. Fold in the pasta and green beans. Put the lid on and cook on high for 20 minutes or until the vegetable are soft and the pasta is al dente.
4. Pour them in a large serving bowl and spread with Parmesan cheese before serving.

Nutrition Info:

- Info Per Serving: Calories: 349;Fat: 6.7g;Protein: 16.5g;Carbs: 59.9g.

Sides , Salads, And Soups Recipes

Bean & Zucchini Soup

Servings:4
Cooking Time:40 Minutes
Ingredients:

- 1 tbsp olive oil
- 1 onion, chopped
- 2 cloves garlic, minced
- 5 cups vegetable broth
- 1 cup dried chickpeas
- ½ cup pinto beans, soaked
- ½ cup navy beans, soaked
- 3 carrots, chopped
- 1 large celery stalk, chopped
- 1 tsp dried thyme
- 16 oz zucchini noodles
- Salt and black pepper to taste

Directions:

1. Warm the olive oil on Sauté in your Instant Pot. Stir in garlic and onion and cook for 5 minutes until golden brown. Mix in pepper, broth, carrots, salt, pepper, celery, beans, chickpeas, and thyme. Seal the lid and cook for 15 minutes on High Pressure. Release the pressure naturally for 10 minutes. Mix zucchini noodles into the soup and stir until wilted. Serve.

Nutrition Info:

- Info Per Serving: Calories: 481;Fat: 8g;Protein: 23g;Carbs: 83g.

Tomato & Apple Salad With Walnuts

Servings:4
Cooking Time:5 Minutes
Ingredients:

- 2 tbsp olive oil
- 1 apple, peeled and chopped
- 1 head Iceberg lettuce, torn
- 1 tbsp apple cider vinegar
- 2 tbsp walnuts, chopped
- 1 tomato, sliced
- 8 anchovy stuffed olives
- Salt to taste

Directions:

1. Combine lettuce, apple cider vinegar, salt, olive oil, apple, and walnuts in a salad bowl. Toss to coat. Top with tomato and olives and serve right away.

Nutrition Info:

- Info Per Serving: Calories: 160;Fat: 2g;Protein: 3g;Carbs: 4g.

Butternut Squash And Cauliflower Curry Soup

Servings:4
Cooking Time: 4 Hours
Ingredients:

- 1 pound butternut squash, peeled and cut into 1-inch cubes
- 1 small head cauliflower, cut into 1-inch pieces
- 1 onion, sliced
- 2 cups unsweetened coconut milk
- 1 tablespoon curry powder
- ½ cup no-added-sugar apple juice
- 4 cups low-sodium vegetable soup
- 2 tablespoons coconut oil
- 1 teaspoon sea salt
- ¼ teaspoon freshly ground white pepper
- ¼ cup chopped fresh cilantro, divided

Directions:

1. Combine all the ingredients, except for the cilantro, in the slow cooker. Stir to mix well.
2. Cook on high heat for 4 hours or until the vegetables are tender.
3. Pour the soup in a food processor, then pulse until creamy and smooth.
4. Pour the puréed soup in a large serving bowl and garnish with cilantro before serving.

Nutrition Info:

- Info Per Serving: Calories: 415;Fat: 30.8g;Protein: 10.1g;Carbs: 29.9g.

Baby Spinach & Apple Salad With Walnuts

Servings:4
Cooking Time:5 Minutes
Ingredients:

- 2 oz sharp white cheddar cheese, cubed
- 3 tbsp olive oil
- 8 cups baby spinach
- 1 Granny Smith apple, diced
- 1 medium red apple, diced
- ½ cup toasted pecans
- 1 tbsp apple cider vinegar

Directions:

1. Toss the spinach, apples, pecans, and cubed cheese together. Lightly drizzle olive oil and vinegar over the top and serve.

Nutrition Info:

- Info Per Serving: Calories: 138;Fat: 12.8g;Protein: 1g;Carbs: 7g.

Chicken & Barley Soup

Servings:4
Cooking Time:40 Minutes
Ingredients:

- 2 tbsp olive oil
- 1 lb boneless chicken thighs
- ¼ cup pearl barley
- 1 red onion, chopped
- 2 cloves garlic, minced
- 4 cups chicken broth
- ¼ tsp oregano
- ½ lemon, juiced
- ¼ tsp parsley
- ¼ cup scallions, chopped
- Salt and black pepper to taste

Directions:

1. Heat the olive oil in a pot over medium heat and sweat the onion and garlic for 2-3 minutes until tender. Place in chicken thighs and cook for 5-6 minutes, stirring often.

2. Pour in chicken broth and barley and bring to a boil. Then lower the heat and simmer for 5 minutes. Remove the chicken and shred it with two forks. Return to the pot and add in lemon, oregano, and parsley. Simmer for 20-22 more minutes. Stir in shredded chicken and adjust the seasoning. Divide between 4 bowls and top with chopped scallions.

Nutrition Info:

- Info Per Serving: Calories: 373;Fat: 17g;Protein: 39g;Carbs: 14g.

Whipped Feta Spread

Servings:6
Cooking Time:10 Minutes
Ingredients:

- 4 tbsp Greek yogurt
- ½ lb feta cheese, crumbled
- 3 cloves garlic, pressed
- 2 tbsp extra-virgin olive oil
- 2 tbsp finely chopped dill
- 1 tsp dried oregano
- Black pepper to taste

Directions:

1. Combine feta, yogurt, garlic, olive oil, and oregano in your food processor. Pulse until well combined. Keep in the fridge until required. To serve, spoon into a dish and sprinkle with dill and black pepper.

Nutrition Info:

- Info Per Serving: Calories: 155;Fat: 13g;Protein: 6g;Carbs: 4g.

Italian Tuna & Bean Salad

Servings:4
Cooking Time:10 Minutes
Ingredients:

- 2 cans can tuna packed in olive oil, drained and flaked
- 4 cups spring mix greens
- 1 can cannellini beans
- ⅔ cup feta cheese, crumbled
- 6 sun-dried tomatoes, sliced
- 10 Kalamata olives, sliced
- 2 thinly sliced green onions
- ¼ medium red onion, sliced
- 3 tbsp extra-virgin olive oil
- ½ tsp dried cilantro
- 3 leaves fresh basil, chopped
- 1 lemon, zested and juiced
- Salt and black pepper to taste

Directions:

1. Place the greens, cannellini beans, tuna, feta, tomatoes, olives, green onions, red onion, olive oil, cilantro, basil, and lemon juice and zest in a large bowl. Season with salt and pepper and mix to coat. Serve and enjoy!

Nutrition Info:

- Info Per Serving: Calories: 354;Fat: 19g;Protein: 22g;Carbs: 25g.

Herby Yogurt Sauce

Servings:4
Cooking Time:5 Minutes
Ingredients:

- ¼ tsp fresh lemon juice
- 1 cup plain yogurt
- 2 tbsp fresh cilantro, minced
- 2 tbsp fresh mint, minced
- 1 garlic clove, minced
- Salt and black pepper to taste

Directions:

1. Place the lemon juice, yogurt, cilantro, mint, and garlic together in a bowl and mix well. Season with salt and pepper. Let sit for about 30 minutes to blend the flavors. Store in an airtight container in the refrigerator for up to 2-3 days.

Nutrition Info:

- Info Per Serving: Calories: 46;Fat: 0.8g;Protein: 3.6g;Carbs: 4.8g.

Collard Green & Rice Salad

Servings:4
Cooking Time:10 Minutes
Ingredients:

- 1 tbsp olive oil
- 1 cup white rice
- 10 oz collard greens, torn
- 4 tbsp walnuts, chopped
- 2 tbsp balsamic vinegar
- 4 tbsp tahini paste
- Salt and black pepper to taste
- 2 tbsp parsley, chopped

Directions:

1. Bring to a boil salted water over medium heat. Add in the rice and cook for 15-18 minutes. Drain and rest to cool.
2. Whisk tahini, 4 tbsp of cold water, and vinegar in a bowl. In a separate bowl, combine cooled rice, collard greens, walnuts, salt, pepper, olive oil, and tahini dressing. Serve topped with parsley.

Nutrition Info:

- Info Per Serving: Calories: 180;Fat: 4g;Protein: 4g;Carbs: 6g.

Carrot & Tomato Salad With Cilantro

Servings:4
Cooking Time:10 Minutes
Ingredients:

- 2 tbsp olive oil
- 4 tomatoes, chopped
- 1 carrot, grated
- ¼ cup lime juice
- 1 garlic clove, minced
- Salt and black pepper to taste
- 1 lettuce head, chopped
- 2 green onions, chopped
- ½ cup cilantro, chopped

Directions:

1. Toss lime juice, garlic, salt, pepper, olive oil, carrot, lettuce, onions, tomatoes, cilantro in a bowl. Serve cold.

Nutrition Info:

- Info Per Serving: Calories: 120;Fat: 4g;Protein: 3g;Carbs: 4g.

Creamy Tomato Hummus Soup

Servings:4
Cooking Time:10 Minutes
Ingredients:

- 1 can diced tomatoes
- 1 cup traditional hummus
- 4 cups chicken stock
- ¼ cup basil leaves, sliced
- 1 cup garlic croutons

Directions:

1. Place the tomatoes, hummus, and chicken stock in your blender and blend until smooth. Pour the mixture into a saucepan over medium heat and bring it to a boil. Pour the soup into bowls. Sprinkle with basil and serve with croutons.

Nutrition Info:

- Info Per Serving: Calories: 148;Fat: 6.2g;Protein: 5g;Carbs: 18.8g.

Bell Pepper, Tomato & Egg Salad

Servings:4
Cooking Time:15 Min + Chilling Time
Ingredients:

- 4 tbsp olive oil
- 2 hard-boiled eggs, chopped
- 2 cups Greek yogurt
- 1 cup tomatoes, chopped
- 2 mixed bell peppers, sliced
- 1 yellow onion, thinly sliced
- ½ tsp fresh garlic, minced
- 10 Kalamata olives, sliced
- 3 sun-dried tomatoes, chopped
- 1 tbsp fresh lemon juice
- 1 tsp dill, chopped
- 2 tbsp fresh parsley, chopped
- Salt and black pepper to taste

Directions:

1. In a bowl, combine the bell peppers, onion, garlic, Kalamata olives, chopped tomatoes, and sun-dried tomatoes. Stir in the chopped eggs. For the dressing, combine the lemon juice, olive oil, Greek yogurt, dill, salt, and black pepper in a bowl. Pour over the salad and transfer to the fridge to chill. Serve garnished with olives and parsley.

Nutrition Info:

- Info Per Serving: Calories: 279;Fat: 19g;Protein: 14g;Carbs: 14g.

Homemade Lebanese Bulgur Salad

Servings:4
Cooking Time:20 Min + Cooling Time
Ingredients:

- ½ cup olive oil
- 2 cups fresh parsley, chopped
- ¼ cup mint leaves, chopped
- ½ cup bulgur
- 4 tomatoes, chopped
- 4 spring onions, chopped
- 1 tbsp lemon juice
- 2 tsp sumac
- Salt and black pepper to taste

Directions:

1. Place 1 cup of water in a pot over medium heat and bring to a boil. Add in the bulgur and cook for 10-12 minutes. Let chill in a bowl. When cooled, stir in tomatoes, spring onions, sumac, black pepper, and salt. Drizzle with lemon juice and olive oil and toss to coat. Top with mint and parsley to serve.

Nutrition Info:

- Info Per Serving: Calories: 451;Fat: 27g;Protein: 11g;Carbs: 48g.

Cilantro-tomato Soup

Servings:6
Cooking Time:30 Minutes
Ingredients:

- 2 tbsp olive oil
- 1 onion, chopped
- 3 garlic cloves, minced
- 8 large tomatoes, chopped
- 1 tsp paprika
- 1 tsp ground cumin
- 6 cups chicken broth
- Salt and black pepper to taste
- 1 cup half-and-half
- 2 tbsp chopped cilantro

Directions:

1. Warm the olive oil in a large pot over medium heat. Add the onion and garlic and cook until soft and translucent, 3 minutes. Stir in paprika, cumin, salt, and pepper for 1 minute. Pour in the tomatoes and chicken broth. Simmer for 15 minutes. Puree the soup with an immersion blender. Stir in half-and-half and serve garnished with cilantro.

Nutrition Info:

- Info Per Serving: Calories: 155;Fat: 6g;Protein: 5g;Carbs: 23g.

Spring Salad With Mustard Dressing

Servings:4
Cooking Time:5 Minutes
Ingredients:

- 4 cups spring mix salad greens
- ¼ cup cherry tomatoes
- 1 tbsp fresh parsley, chopped
- 3 tbsp extra-virgin olive oil
- 1 tbsp wine vinegar
- 2 tbsp minced shallots
- ½ tsp yogurt
- ½ tsp Dijon mustard
- Salt and black pepper to taste

Directions:

1. Place parsley, vinegar, shallots, yogurt, mustard, salt, and pepper in a bowl and mix until smooth. Whisking constantly, slowly drizzle in oil until emulsified. In a bowl, combine the salad greens and tomatoes. Pour the dressing over and serve.

Nutrition Info:

- Info Per Serving: Calories: 64;Fat: 4.1g;Protein: 0.6g;Carbs: 2.2g.

Green Bean & Rice Chicken Soup

Servings:4
Cooking Time:45 Minutes
Ingredients:

- 2 tbsp olive oil
- 4 cups chicken stock
- ½ lb chicken breasts strips
- 1 celery stalk, chopped
- 2 garlic cloves, minced
- 1 yellow onion, chopped
- ½ cup white rice
- 1 egg, whisked
- ½ lemon, juiced
- 1 cup green beans, chopped
- 1 cup carrots, chopped
- ½ cup dill, chopped
- Salt and black pepper to taste

Directions:

1. Warm the olive oil in a pot over medium heat and sauté onion, garlic, celery, carrots, and chicken for 6-7 minutes.
2. Pour in stock and rice. Bring to a boil and simmer for 10 minutes. Stir in green beans, salt, and pepper and cook for 15 minutes. Whisk the egg and lemon juice and pour into the pot. Stir and cook for 2 minutes. Serve topped with dill.

Nutrition Info:

- Info Per Serving: Calories: 270;Fat: 19g;Protein: 15g;Carbs: 20g.

Marinated Mushrooms And Olives

Servings:8
Cooking Time: 0 Minutes
Ingredients:

- 1 pound white button mushrooms, rinsed and drained
- 1 pound fresh olives
- ½ tablespoon crushed fennel seeds
- 1 tablespoon white wine vinegar
- 2 tablespoons fresh thyme leaves
- Pinch chili flakes
- Sea salt and freshly ground pepper, to taste
- 2 tablespoons extra-virgin olive oil

Directions:

1. Combine all the ingredients in a large bowl. Toss to mix well.
2. Wrap the bowl in plastic and refrigerate for at least 1 hour to marinate.
3. Remove the bowl from the refrigerate and let sit under room temperature for 10 minutes, then serve.

Nutrition Info:

- Info Per Serving: Calories: 111;Fat: 9.7g;Protein: 2.4g;Carbs: 5.9g.

Homemade Herbes De Provence Spice

Servings:4
Cooking Time:5 Minutes
Ingredients:

- 2 tbsp dried oregano
- 2 tbsp dried thyme
- 2 tbsp dried marjoram
- 2 tbsp dried rosemary
- 2 tsp fennel seeds, toasted

Directions:

1. Mix the oregano, thyme, marjoram, rosemary, and fennel seeds in a bowl. Store the spices in an airtight container at room temperature for up to 7-9 months.

Nutrition Info:

- Info Per Serving: Calories: 32;Fat: 1.1g;Protein: 1.4g;Carbs: 6.0g.

Barley, Parsley, And Pea Salad

Servings:4
Cooking Time: 10 Minutes
Ingredients:

- 2 cups water
- 1 cup quick-cooking barley
- 1 small bunch flat-leaf parsley, chopped
- 2 cups sugar snap pea pods
- Juice of 1 lemon
- ½ small red onion, diced
- 2 tablespoons extra-virgin olive oil
- Sea salt and freshly ground pepper, to taste

Directions:

1. Pour the water in a saucepan. Bring to a boil. Add the barley to the saucepan, then put the lid on.
2. Reduce the heat to low. Simmer the barley for 10 minutes or until the liquid is absorbed, then let sit for 5 minutes.
3. Open the lid, then transfer the barley in a colander and rinse under cold running water.
4. Pour the barley in a large salad bowl and add the remaining ingredients. Toss to combine well.
5. Serve immediately.

Nutrition Info:

- Info Per Serving: Calories: 152;Fat: 7.4g;Protein: 3.7g;Carbs: 19.3g.

Balsamic Brussels Sprouts And Delicata Squash

Servings:2
Cooking Time: 30 Minutes
Ingredients:
- ½ pound Brussels sprouts, ends trimmed and outer leaves removed
- 1 medium delicata squash, halved lengthwise, seeded, and cut into 1-inch pieces
- 1 cup fresh cranberries
- 2 teaspoons olive oil
- Salt and freshly ground black pepper, to taste
- ½ cup balsamic vinegar
- 2 tablespoons roasted pumpkin seeds
- 2 tablespoons fresh pomegranate arils (seeds)

Directions:
1. Preheat oven to 400°F. Line a sheet pan with parchment paper.
2. Combine the Brussels sprouts, squash, and cranberries in a large bowl. Drizzle with olive oil, and season lightly with salt and pepper. Toss well to coat and arrange in a single layer on the sheet pan.
3. Roast in the preheated oven for 30 minutes, turning vegetables halfway through, or until Brussels sprouts turn brown and crisp in spots.
4. Meanwhile, make the balsamic glaze by simmering the vinegar for 10 to 12 minutes, or until mixture has reduced to about ¼ cup and turns a syrupy consistency.
5. Remove the vegetables from the oven, drizzle with balsamic syrup, and sprinkle with pumpkin seeds and pomegranate arils before serving.

Nutrition Info:
- Info Per Serving: Calories: 203;Fat: 6.8g;Protein: 6.2g;Carbs: 22.0g.

Vegetarian Mediterranean Stew

Servings:4
Cooking Time:25 Minutes
Ingredients:
- 1 can garbanzo beans, drained and rinsed
- 1 can cannellini beans, drained and rinsed
- 1 ½ cups artichoke hearts, quartered
- 2 cups roasted tomatoes
- 3 tbsp olive oil
- 3 garlic cloves minced
- 1 cup spinach, chopped
- 1 cup vegetable broth
- 4 tbsp Parmesan, grated
- 1 tsp red pepper flakes
- 1 tsp dried oregano
- Salt and black pepper to taste
- 4 sun-dried tomatoes, chopped
- 1 tbsp parsley, chopped
- 1 cup garlic-seasoned croutons
- 2 tbsp feta cheese, crumbled
- 1 tbsp oregano, chopped

Directions:
1. Warm the olive oil in a pot over medium heat and sauté the garlic for 2–3 minutes until golden. Lower the heat to low. Add in the garbanzo beans, cannellini beans, roasted tomatoes, artichoke hearts, spinach, broth, Parmesan cheese, red pepper flakes, oregano, salt, and pepper. Cook and stir for about 10 minutes. Serve warm in individual bowls garnished with sun-dried tomatoes, parsley, croutons, feta cheese, and oregano.

Nutrition Info:
- Info Per Serving: Calories: 452;Fat: 16g;Protein: 21g;Carbs: 65g.

Arugula & Fruit Salad

Servings:4
Cooking Time:5 Minutes
Ingredients:
- 6 figs, quartered
- 2 cups arugula
- 1 cup strawberries, halved
- 1 tbsp hemp seeds
- 1 cucumber, sliced
- 1 tbsp lime juice
- 1 tbsp tahini paste

Directions:
1. Spread the arugula on a serving plate. Top with strawberries, figs, and cucumber. In another bowl, whisk tahini, hemp seeds, and lime juice and pour over the salad. Serve.

Nutrition Info:
- Info Per Serving: Calories: 220;Fat: 5g;Protein: 4g;Carbs: 11g.

Cherry & Pine Nut Couscous

Servings:6
Cooking Time:10 Minutes
Ingredients:
- 2 tbsp olive oil
- 3 cups hot water
- 1 cup couscous
- ½ cup pine nuts, roasted
- ½ cup dry cherries, chopped
- ½ cup parsley, chopped
- Salt and black pepper to taste
- 1 tbsp lime juice

Directions:
1. Place couscous and hot water in a bowl and let sit for 10 minutes. Fluff with a fork and remove to a bowl. Stir in pine nuts, cherries, parsley, salt, pepper, lime juice, and olive oil.

Nutrition Info:
- Info Per Serving: Calories: 220;Fat: 8g;Protein: 6g;Carbs: 9g.

Green Beans With Tahini-lemon Sauce

Servings:2
Cooking Time: 10 Minutes
Ingredients:
- 1 pound green beans, washed and trimmed
- 2 tablespoons tahini
- 1 garlic clove, minced
- Grated zest and juice of 1 lemon
- Salt and black pepper, to taste
- 1 teaspoon toasted black or white sesame seeds (optional)

Directions:
1. Steam the beans in a medium saucepan fitted with a steamer basket (or by adding ¼ cup water to a covered saucepan) over medium-high heat. Drain, reserving the cooking water.
2. Mix the tahini, garlic, lemon zest and juice, and salt and pepper to taste. Use the reserved cooking water to thin the sauce as desired.
3. Toss the green beans with the sauce and garnish with the sesame seeds, if desired. Serve immediately.

Nutrition Info:
- Info Per Serving: Calories: 188;Fat: 8.4g;Protein: 7.2g;Carbs: 22.2g.

Pumpkin Soup With Crispy Sage Leaves

Servings:4
Cooking Time: 10 Minutes

Ingredients:

- 1 tablespoon olive oil
- 2 garlic cloves, cut into ⅛-inch-thick slices
- 1 onion, chopped
- 2 cups freshly puréed pumpkin
- 4 cups low-sodium vegetable soup
- 2 teaspoons chipotle powder
- 1 teaspoon sea salt
- ½ teaspoon freshly ground black pepper
- ½ cup vegetable oil
- 12 sage leaves, stemmed

Directions:

1. Heat the olive oil in a stockpot over high heat until shimmering.
2. Add the garlic and onion, then sauté for 5 minutes or until the onion is translucent.
3. Pour in the puréed pumpkin and vegetable soup in the pot, then sprinkle with chipotle powder, salt, and ground black pepper. Stir to mix well.
4. Bring to a boil. Reduce the heat to low and simmer for 5 minutes.
5. Meanwhile, heat the vegetable oil in a nonstick skillet over high heat.
6. Add the sage leaf to the skillet and sauté for a minute or until crispy. Transfer the sage on paper towels to soak the excess oil.
7. Gently pour the soup in three serving bowls, then divide the crispy sage leaves in bowls for garnish. Serve immediately.

Nutrition Info:

- Info Per Serving: Calories: 380;Fat: 20.1g;Protein: 8.9g;Carbs: 45.2g.

Fruits, Desserts And Snacks Recipes

Turkey Pesto Pizza

Servings:4
Cooking Time:35 Minutes
Ingredients:
- Pizza Crust
- 3 tbsp olive oil
- 3 cups flour
- ¼ tsp salt
- 3 large eggs
- Topping
- ½ lb turkey ham, chopped
- 2 tbsp cashew nuts
- 1 green bell pepper, sliced
- 1 ½ cups basil pesto
- 1 cup mozzarella, grated
- 2 tbsp Parmesan cheese, grated
- 4 fresh basil leaves, chopped
- ¼ tsp red pepper flakes

Directions:
1. In a bowl, mix flour, olive oil, salt, and egg until a dough forms. Mold the dough into a ball and place it in between two full parchment papers on a flat surface. Roll it out into a circle of a ¼ -inch thickness. After, slide the pizza dough into the pizza pan and remove the parchment paper. Place the pizza pan in the oven and bake the dough for 20 minutes at 350 °F. Once the pizza bread is ready, remove it from the oven, fold and seal the extra inch of dough at its edges to make a crust around it. Apply 2/3 of the pesto on it and sprinkle half of the mozzarella cheese too.
2. Toss the chopped turkey ham in the remaining pesto and spread it on top of the pizza. Sprinkle with the remaining mozzarella, bell peppers, and cashew nuts and put the pizza back in the oven to bake for 9 minutes. When it is ready, remove from the oven to cool slightly, garnish with the basil leaves and sprinkle with parmesan cheese and red pepper flakes. Slice and serve.

Nutrition Info:
- Info Per Serving: Calories: 684;Fat: 54g;Protein: 32g;Carbs: 22g.

Mint-watermelon Gelato

Servings:4
Cooking Time:10 Min + Freezing Time
Ingredients:
- ¼ cup honey
- 4 cups watermelon cubes
- ¼ cup lemon juice
- 12 mint leaves to serve

Directions:
1. In a food processor, blend the watermelon, honey, and lemon juice to form a purée with chunks. Transfer to a freezer-proof container and place in the freezer for 1 hour.
2. Remove the container from and scrape with a fork. Return the to the freezer and repeat the process every half hour until the sorbet is completely frozen, for around 4 hours. Share into bowls, garnish with mint leaves, and serve.

Nutrition Info:
- Info Per Serving: Calories: 149;Fat: 0.4g;Protein: 1.8g;Carbs: 38g.

Bean & Artichoke Dip

Servings:4
Cooking Time:10 Minutes
Ingredients:

- 2 tbsp olive oil
- 15 oz canned Cannellini beans
- 1 red onion, chopped
- 6 oz canned artichoke hearts,
- 4 garlic cloves, minced
- 1 tbsp thyme, chopped
- ½ lemon, juiced and zested
- Salt and black pepper to taste

Directions:

1. Warm olive oil in a skillet over medium heat and sauté onion and garlic for 4-5 minutes until translucent. Add in the artichoke hearts and cook for 2-3 more minutes. Set aside to cool slightly. Transfer the cooled mixture to a blender along with cannellini beans, thyme, lemon juice, lemon zest, salt, and pepper and blitz until it becomes smooth. Serve.

Nutrition Info:

- Info Per Serving: Calories: 280;Fat: 12g;Protein: 17g;Carbs: 19g.

Spiced Nut Mix

Servings:6
Cooking Time:20 Minutes
Ingredients:

- 1 tbsp olive oil
- 2 cups raw mixed nuts
- 1 tsp ground cumin
- ½ tsp garlic powder
- ½ tsp kosher salt
- ⅛ tsp chili powder
- ⅛ tsp ground coriander

Directions:

1. Place the nuts in a skillet over medium heat and toast for 3 minutes, shaking the pan continuously. Remove to a bowl, season with salt, and reserve. Warm olive oil in the same skillet. Add in cumin, garlic powder, chili powder, and ground coriander and cook for about 20-30 seconds. Mix in nuts and cook for another 4 minutes. Serve chilled.

Nutrition Info:

- Info Per Serving: Calories: 315;Fat: 29.2g;Protein: 8g;Carbs: 11g.

Turkish Baklava

Servings:6
Cooking Time:40 Min + Chilling Time
Ingredients:

- 20 sheets phyllo pastry dough, at room temperature
- 1 cup butter, melted
- 1 ½ cups chopped walnuts
- 1 tsp ground cinnamon
- ¼ tsp ground cardamom
- ½ cup sugar
- ½ cup honey
- 2 tbsp lemon juice
- 1 tbsp lemon zest

Directions:

1. In a small pot, bring 1 cup of water, sugar, honey, lemon zest, and lemon juice just to a boil. Remove and let cool.
2. Preheat oven to 350 °F. In a small bowl, mix the walnuts, cinnamon, and cardamom and set aside. Put the butter in a small bowl. Put 1 layer of phyllo dough on a baking sheet and slowly brush with butter. Carefully layer 2 more phyllo sheets, brushing each with butter in the baking pan and then layer 1 tbsp of the nut mix; layer 2 sheets and add another 1 tbsp of the nut mix; repeat with 2 sheets and nuts until you run out of nuts and dough, topping with the remaining phyllo dough sheets. Slice 4 lines into the baklava lengthwise and make another 4 or 5 slices diagonally across the pan. Bake for 30-40 minutes or until golden brown. Remove the baklava from the oven and immediately cover it with the syrup. Let cool and serve.

Nutrition Info:

- Info Per Serving: Calories: 443;Fat: 27g;Protein: 6g;Carbs: 47g.

Basic Pudding With Kiwi

Servings:4
Cooking Time:20 Min + Chilling Time
Ingredients:

- 2 kiwi, peeled and sliced
- 1 egg
- 2 ¼ cups milk
- ½ cup honey
- 1 tsp vanilla extract
- 3 tbsp cornstarch

Directions:

1. In a bowl, beat the egg with honey. Stir in 2 cups of milk and vanilla. Pour into a pot over medium heat and bring to a boil. Combine cornstarch and remaining milk in a bowl. Pour slowly into the pot and boil for 1 minute until thickened, stirring often. Divide between 4 cups and transfer to the fridge. Top with kiwi and serve.

Nutrition Info:

- Info Per Serving: Calories: 262;Fat: 4.1g;Protein: 6.5g;Carbs: 52g.

Roasted Carrot Ribbons With Mayo Sauce

Servings:4
Cooking Time:50 Minutes
Ingredients:

- 2 tbsp olive oil
- 1 lb carrots, shaved into ribbons
- Salt and black pepper to taste
- ½ lemon, zested
- 1/3 cup light mayonnaise
- 1 garlic clove, minced
- 1 tsp cumin, ground
- 1 tbsp dill, chopped

Directions:

1. Preheat the oven to 380 °F. Spread carrot ribbons on a paper-lined roasting tray. Drizzle with some olive oil and sprinkle with cumin, salt, and pepper. Roast for 20-25 minutes until crisp and golden. In a bowl, mix mayonnaise, lemon zest, garlic, dill, and remaining olive oil. Serve the roasted carrots with mayo sauce.

Nutrition Info:

- Info Per Serving: Calories: 200;Fat: 6g;Protein: 6g;Carbs: 8g.

Cucumber Noodles With Goat Cheese

Servings:4
Cooking Time:5 Minutes
Ingredients:

- ½ cup olive oil
- 2 cucumbers, spiralized
- ½ cup black olives, sliced
- 12 cherry tomatoes, halved
- Salt and black pepper to taste
- 1 small red onion, chopped
- ½ cup goat cheese, crumbled
- ¼ cup apple cider vinegar

Directions:

1. Combine olives, tomatoes, salt, pepper, onion, goat cheese, olive oil, and vinegar in a bowl and mix well. Place the cucumbers on a platter and top with the cheese mixture.

Nutrition Info:

- Info Per Serving: Calories: 150;Fat: 15g;Protein: 2g;Carbs: 4g.

Orange Mug Cakes

Servings:2
Cooking Time: 3 Minutes
Ingredients:
- 6 tablespoons flour
- 2 tablespoons sugar
- 1 teaspoon orange zest
- ½ teaspoon baking powder
- Pinch salt
- 1 egg
- 2 tablespoons olive oil
- 2 tablespoons unsweetened almond milk
- 2 tablespoons freshly squeezed orange juice
- ½ teaspoon orange extract
- ½ teaspoon vanilla extract

Directions:
1. Combine the flour, sugar, orange zest, baking powder, and salt in a small bowl.
2. In another bowl, whisk together the egg, olive oil, milk, orange juice, orange extract, and vanilla extract.
3. Add the dry ingredients to the wet ingredients and stir to incorporate. The batter will be thick.
4. Divide the mixture into two small mugs. Microwave each mug separately. The small ones should take about 60 seconds, and one large mug should take about 90 seconds, but microwaves can vary.
5. Cool for 5 minutes before serving.

Nutrition Info:
- Info Per Serving: Calories: 303;Fat: 16.9g;Protein: 6.0g;Carbs: 32.5g.

Cheese Stuffed Potato Skins

Servings:4
Cooking Time:40 Minutes
Ingredients:
- 2 tbsp olive oil
- 1 lb red baby potatoes
- 1 cup ricotta cheese, crumbled
- 2 garlic cloves, minced
- 1 tbsp chives, chopped
- ½ tsp hot chili sauce
- Salt and black pepper to taste

Directions:
1. Place potatoes and enough water in a pot over medium heat and bring to a boil. Simmer for 15 minutes and drain. Let them cool. Cut them in halves and scoop out the pulp. Place the pulp in a bowl and mash it a bit with a fork. Add in the ricotta cheese, olive oil, garlic, chives, chili sauce, salt, and pepper. Mix to combine. Fill potato skins with the mixture.
2. Preheat oven to 360 °F. Line a baking sheet with parchment paper. Place filled skins on the sheet and bake for 10 minutes.

Nutrition Info:
- Info Per Serving: Calories: 310;Fat: 10g;Protein: 9g;Carbs: 23g.

Speedy Granita

Servings:4
Cooking Time:10 Min + Freezing Time
Ingredients:

- ¼ cup sugar
- 1 cup fresh strawberries
- 1 cup fresh raspberries
- 1 cup chopped fresh kiwi
- 1 tsp lemon juice

Directions:
1. Bring 1 cup water to a boil in a small saucepan over high heat. Add the sugar and stir well until dissolved. Remove the pan from the heat, add the fruit and lemon juice, and cool to room temperature. Once cooled, puree the fruit in a blender until smooth. Pour the puree into a shallow glass baking dish and place in the freezer for 1 hour. Stir with a fork and freeze for 30 minutes, then repeat. Serve and enjoy!

Nutrition Info:
- Info Per Serving: Calories: 153;Fat: 0.2g;Protein: 1.6g;Carbs: 39g.

Vegetarian Patties

Servings:4
Cooking Time:20 Minutes
Ingredients:

- 3 tbsp olive oil
- 2 carrots, grated
- 2 zucchinis, grated and drained
- 2 garlic cloves, minced
- 2 spring onions, chopped
- 1 tsp cumin
- ½ tsp turmeric powder
- Salt and black pepper to taste
- ¼ tsp ground coriander
- 2 tbsp parsley, chopped
- ¼ tsp lemon juice
- ½ cup flour
- 1 egg, whisked
- ¼ cup breadcrumbs

Directions:
1. Combine garlic, spring onions, carrot, cumin, turmeric, salt, pepper, coriander, parsley, lemon juice, flour, zucchinis, egg, and breadcrumbs in a bowl and mix well. Form balls out of the mixture and flatten them to form patties.
2. Warm olive oil in a skillet over medium heat. Fry the cakes for 10 minutes on both sides. Remove to a paper-lined plate to drain the excessive grease. Serve warm.

Nutrition Info:
- Info Per Serving: Calories: 220;Fat: 12g;Protein: 5g;Carbs: 5g.

Olive Mezze Platter

Servings:2
Cooking Time:10 Min + Marinating Time
Ingredients:

- 2 cups mixed green olives with pits
- ¼ cup extra-virgin olive oil
- ¼ cup red wine vinegar
- 1 tsp dried oregano
- 1 orange, zested and juiced
- ½ tsp crushed chilies
- ½ tsp ground cumin

Directions:
1. Combine the olives, vinegar, olive oil, garlic, oregano, crushed chilies, and cumin in a large glass and mix well. Cover and set aside to marinate for 30 minutes. Keep for up to 14 days in the refrigerator.

Nutrition Info:
- Info Per Serving: Calories: 133;Fat: 14g;Protein: 1g;Carbs: 3g.

Cardamom Apple Slices

Servings:2
Cooking Time:30 Minutes
Ingredients:
- 1 ½ tsp cardamom
- ½ tsp salt
- 4 peeled, cored apples, sliced
- 2 tbsp honey
- 2 tbsp milk

Directions:
1. Preheat oven to 390 °F. In a bowl, combine apple slices, salt, and ½ tsp of cardamom. Arrange them on a greased baking dish and cook for 20 minutes. Remove to a serving plate.
2. In the meantime, place milk, honey, and remaining cardamom in a pot over medium heat. Cook until simmer. Pour the sauce over the apples and serve immediately.

Nutrition Info:
- Info Per Serving: Calories: 287;Fat: 3g;Protein: 2g;Carbs: 69g.

Energy Granola Bites

Servings:5
Cooking Time:10 Minutes
Ingredients:
- ¾ cup diced dried figs
- ½ cup chopped walnuts
- ¼ cup old-fashioned oats
- 2 tbsp ground flaxseed
- 2 tbsp peanut butter
- 2 tbsp honey

Directions:
1. In a medium bowl, mix together the figs, walnuts, oats, flaxseed, and peanut butter. Drizzle with the honey, and mix everything with a wooden spoon. Freeze the dough for 5 minutes. Divide the dough evenly into four sections in the bowl. Dampen your hands with water—but don't get them too wet, or the dough will stick to them. With hands, roll three bites out of each of the four sections of dough, making 10 energy bites. Store in the fridge for up to a week.

Nutrition Info:
- Info Per Serving: Calories: 158;Fat: 8g;Protein: 3g;Carbs: 23g.

Berry And Rhubarb Cobbler

Servings:8
Cooking Time: 35 Minutes
Ingredients:

- Cobbler:
- 1 cup fresh raspberries
- 2 cups fresh blueberries
- 1 cup sliced (½-inch) rhubarb pieces
- 1 tablespoon arrowroot powder
- ¼ cup unsweetened apple juice
- 2 tablespoons melted coconut oil
- ¼ cup raw honey
- Topping:
- 1 cup almond flour
- 1 tablespoon arrowroot powder
- ½ cup shredded coconut
- ¼ cup raw honey
- ½ cup coconut oil

Directions:

1. Make the Cobbler
2. Preheat the oven to 350ºF. Grease a baking dish with melted coconut oil.
3. Combine the ingredients for the cobbler in a large bowl. Stir to mix well.
4. Spread the mixture in the single layer on the baking dish. Set aside.
5. Make the Topping
6. Combine the almond flour, arrowroot powder, and coconut in a bowl. Stir to mix well.
7. Fold in the honey and coconut oil. Stir with a fork until the mixture crumbled.
8. Spread the topping over the cobbler, then bake in the preheated oven for 35 minutes or until frothy and golden brown.
9. Serve immediately.

Nutrition Info:

- Info Per Serving: Calories: 305;Fat: 22.1g;Protein: 3.2g;Carbs: 29.8g.

Authentic Greek Potato Skins

Servings:4
Cooking Time:1 Hour 10 Minutes
Ingredients:

- 2 tbsp extra-virgin olive oil
- 1 cup feta cheese, crumbled
- 1 lb potatoes
- ½ cup Greek yogurt
- 2 spring onions, chopped
- 3 sundried tomatoes, chopped
- 6 Kalamata olives, chopped
- ½ tsp dried dill
- 1 tsp Greek oregano
- 2 tbsp halloumi cheese, grated
- Salt and black pepper to taste

Directions:

1. Preheat oven to 400 °F. Pierce the potatoes in several places with a fork. Wrap in aluminum foil and bake in the oven for 45-50 minutes until tender. Let cool. Split the cooled potatoes lengthwise and scoop out some of the flesh. Put the flesh in a bowl and mash with a fork.
2. Add in the spring onions, sun-dried tomatoes, olives, dill, oregano, feta cheese, and yogurt and stir. Season with salt and pepper. Fill the potato shells with the feta mixture and top with halloumi cheese. Transfer the boats to a baking sheet and place under the broiler for 5 minutes until the top is golden and crisp. Serve right away.

Nutrition Info:

- Info Per Serving: Calories: 294;Fat: 18g;Protein: 12g;Carbs: 22g.

Coconut Blueberries With Brown Rice

Servings:4
Cooking Time: 10 Minutes
Ingredients:
- 1 cup fresh blueberries
- 2 cups unsweetened coconut milk
- 1 teaspoon ground ginger
- ¼ cup maple syrup
- Sea salt, to taste
- 2 cups cooked brown rice

Directions:
1. Put all the ingredients, except for the brown rice, in a pot. Stir to combine well.
2. Cook over medium-high heat for 7 minutes or until the blueberries are tender.
3. Pour in the brown rice and cook for 3 more minute or until the rice is soft. Stir constantly.
4. Serve immediately.

Nutrition Info:
- Info Per Serving: Calories: 470;Fat: 24.8g;Protein: 6.2g;Carbs: 60.1g.

Garbanzo Patties With Cilantro-yogurt Sauce

Servings:4
Cooking Time:20 Minutes
Ingredients:
- ¼ cup olive oil
- 3 garlic cloves, minced
- 1 cup canned garbanzo beans
- 2 tbsp parsley, chopped
- 1 onion, chopped
- 1 tsp ground coriander
- Salt and black pepper to taste
- ¼ tsp cayenne pepper
- ¼ tsp cumin powder
- 1 tsp lemon juice
- 3 tbsp flour
- ¼ cup Greek yogurt
- 2 tbsp chopped cilantro
- ½ tsp garlic powder

Directions:
1. In a blender, blitz garbanzo, parsley, onion, garlic, salt, pepper, ground coriander, cayenne pepper, cumin powder, and lemon juice until smooth. Remove to a bowl and mix in flour. Form 16 balls out of the mixture and flatten them into patties.
2. Warm the olive oil in a skillet over medium heat and fry patties for 10 minutes on both sides. Remove them to a paper towel–lined plate to drain the excess fat. In a bowl, mix the Greek yogurt, cilantro, garlic powder, salt, and pepper. Serve the patties with yogurt sauce.

Nutrition Info:
- Info Per Serving: Calories: 120;Fat: 7g;Protein: 4g;Carbs: 13g.

Rice Pudding With Roasted Orange

Servings:6
Cooking Time: 19 To 20 Minutes
Ingredients:

- 2 medium oranges
- 2 teaspoons extra-virgin olive oil
- ⅛ teaspoon kosher salt
- 2 large eggs
- 2 cups unsweetened almond milk
- 1 cup orange juice
- 1 cup uncooked instant brown rice
- ¼ cup honey
- ½ teaspoon ground cinnamon
- 1 teaspoon vanilla extract
- Cooking spray

Directions:

1. Preheat the oven to 450ºF. Spritz a large, rimmed baking sheet with cooking spray. Set aside.
2. Slice the unpeeled oranges into ¼-inch rounds. Brush with the oil and sprinkle with salt. Place the slices on the baking sheet and roast for 4 minutes. Flip the slices and roast for 4 more minutes, or until they begin to brown. Remove from the oven and set aside.
3. Crack the eggs into a medium bowl. In a medium saucepan, whisk together the milk, orange juice, rice, honey and cinnamon. Bring to a boil over medium-high heat, stirring constantly. Reduce the heat to medium-low and simmer for 10 minutes, stirring occasionally.
4. Using a measuring cup, scoop out ½ cup of the hot rice mixture and whisk it into the eggs. While constantly stirring the mixture in the pan, slowly pour the egg mixture back into the saucepan. Cook on low heat for 1 to 2 minutes, or until thickened, stirring constantly. Remove from the heat and stir in the vanilla.
5. Let the pudding stand for a few minutes for the rice to soften. The rice will be cooked but slightly chewy. For softer rice, let stand for another half hour.
6. Top with the roasted oranges. Serve warm or at room temperature.

Nutrition Info:

- Info Per Serving: Calories: 204;Fat: 6.0g;Protein: 5.0g;Carbs: 34.0g.

Spiced Hot Chocolate

Servings:4
Cooking Time:15 Minutes
Ingredients:

- ¼ tsp cayenne pepper powder
- 4 squares chocolate
- 4 cups milk
- 2 tsp sugar
- ½ tsp ground cinnamon
- ½ tsp salt

Directions:

1. Place milk and sugar in a pot over low heat and warm until it begins to simmer.
2. Combine chocolate, cinnamon, salt, and cayenne pepper powder in a bowl. Slowly pour in enough hot milk to cover. Return the pot to the heat and lower the temperature. Stir until the chocolate has melted, then add the remaining milk and combine. Spoon into 4 cups and serve hot.

Nutrition Info:

- Info Per Serving: Calories: 342;Fat: 23g;Protein: 12g;Carbs: 22g.

Cointreau Poached Pears

Servings:4
Cooking Time:60 Minutes
Ingredients:
- 4 Bosc pears, peeled
- ¼ tsp cardamom seeds
- 1 cup orange juice
- 1 cinnamon stick
- 1-star anise
- 1 tbsp Cointreau liqueur
- 1 tsp allspice berries
- 1 tsp orange zest
- 3 cups red wine
- 1 cup sugar
- 1 cup whipping cream

Directions:
1. Place orange liqueur and red wine in a pot over medium heat and bring to a boil. Reduce the heat to low and add the cardamom seeds, cinnamon stick, allspice berries, orange juice, orange zest, and star anise; simmer for 5 minutes. Add in the pears and sugar, cover, and poach for about 25-30 minutes until tender.
2. Remove the pears from the pot and set aside. Drain the cooking liquid through a sieve, then return it to the pot. Bring to a boil and cook until the liquid obtains a syrup-like consistency, about 10-15 minutes. Pour the sauce over the pears, top with whipping cream, and serve.

Nutrition Info:
- Info Per Serving: Calories: 226;Fat: 4.6g;Protein: 11.3g;Carbs: 7g.

Healthy Tuna Stuffed Zucchini Rolls

Servings:4
Cooking Time:5 Minutes
Ingredients:
- 5 oz canned tuna, drained and mashed
- 2 tbsp olive oil
- ½ cup mayonnaise
- 2 tbsp capers
- 2 zucchinis, sliced lengthwise
- Salt and black pepper to taste
- 1 tsp lime juice

Directions:
1. Heat a grill pan over medium heat. Drizzle the zucchini slices with olive oil and season with salt and pepper. Grill for 5-6 minutes on both sides. In a bowl, mix the tuna, capers, lime juice, mayonnaise, salt, and pepper until well combined. Spread the tuna mixture onto zucchini slices and roll them up. Transfer the rolls to a plate and serve.

Nutrition Info:
- Info Per Serving: Calories: 210;Fat: 7g;Protein: 4g;Carbs: 8g.

Simple Spiced Sweet Pecans

Servings: 4
Cooking Time: 17 Minutes
Ingredients:
- 1 cup pecan halves
- 3 tablespoons almond butter
- 1 teaspoon ground cinnamon
- ½ teaspoon ground nutmeg
- ¼ cup raw honey
- ¼ teaspoon sea salt

Directions:
1. Preheat the oven to 350°F. Line a baking sheet with parchment paper.
2. Combine all the ingredients in a bowl. Stir to mix well, then spread the mixture in the single layer on the baking sheet with a spatula.
3. Bake in the preheated oven for 16 minutes or until the pecan halves are well browned.
4. Serve immediately.

Nutrition Info:
- Info Per Serving: Calories: 324;Fat: 29.8g;Protein: 3.2g;Carbs: 13.9g.

Hummus & Tomato Stuffed Cucumbers

Servings: 2
Cooking Time: 5 Minutes
Ingredients:
- 1 cucumber, halved lengthwise
- ½ cup hummus
- 5 cherry tomatoes, halved
- 2 tbsp fresh basil, minced

Directions:
1. Using a paring knife, scoop most of the seeds from the inside of each cucumber piece to make a cup, being careful not to cut all the way through. Fill each cucumber cup with about 1 tablespoon of hummus. Top with cherry tomatoes and basil.

Nutrition Info:
- Info Per Serving: Calories: 135;Fat: 6g;Protein: 6g;Carbs: 16g.

28 Day Meal Plan

Day 1
Breakfast: Napoli Scrambled Eggs With Anchovies
Lunch: Italian Tilapia Pilaf
Dinner: Seafood Cakes With Radicchio Salad

Day 2
Breakfast: Fresh Mozzarella & Salmon Frittata
Lunch: Spicy Haddock Stew
Dinner: Roasted Veggies And Brown Rice Bowl

Day 3
Breakfast: Open-faced Margherita Sandwiches
Lunch: Salt And Pepper Calamari And Scallops
Dinner: Vegan Lentil Bolognese

Day 4
Breakfast: Apple & Date Smoothie
Lunch: Prawns With Mushrooms
Dinner: Sautéed Cabbage With Parsley

Day 5
Breakfast: White Pizzas With Arugula And Spinach
Lunch: Juicy Basil-tomato Scallops
Dinner: Grilled Za´atar Zucchini Rounds

Day 6
Breakfast: Brown Rice Salad With Cheese
Lunch: Pan-fried Tuna With Vegetables
Dinner: Celery And Mustard Greens

Day 7
Breakfast: Dulse, Avocado, And Tomato Pitas
Lunch: Parsley Tomato Tilapia
Dinner: Sweet Potato Chickpea Buddha Bowl

Day 8
Breakfast: Anchovy & Spinach Sandwiches
Lunch: Dill Smoked Salmon & Eggplant Rolls
Dinner: Cauliflower Rice Risotto With Mushrooms

Day 9
Breakfast: Falafel Balls With Tahini Sauce
Lunch: Mediterranean Grilled Sea Bass
Dinner: Veggie-stuffed Portabello Mushrooms

Day 10
Breakfast: Baked Ricotta With Honey Pears
Lunch: Salmon And Mushroom Hash With Pesto
Dinner: Parsley & Olive Zucchini Bake

Day 11
Breakfast: Honey & Feta Frozen Yogurt
Lunch: Dill Baked Sea Bass
Dinner: Balsamic Cherry Tomatoes

Day 12
Breakfast: Samosas In Potatoes
Lunch: Parchment Orange & Dill Salmon
Dinner: Garlicky Zucchini Cubes With Mint

Day 13
Breakfast: Luxurious Fruit Cocktail
Lunch: Avocado & Onion Tilapia
Dinner: Wilted Dandelion Greens With Sweet Onion

Day 14
Breakfast: Tomato Eggs With Fried Potatoes
Lunch: Hake Fillet In Herby Tomato Sauce
Dinner: Baked Vegetable Stew

Day 15

Breakfast: Turkish Eggplant And Tomatoes Pide With Mint
Lunch: Shrimp & Salmon In Tomato Sauce
Dinner: Roasted Vegetables And Chickpeas

Day 16

Breakfast: Couscous & Cucumber Bowl
Lunch: Shrimp And Pea Paella
Dinner: Buttery Garlic Green Beans

Day 17

Breakfast: Artichoke & Spinach Frittata
Lunch: Cheesy Smoked Salmon Crostini
Dinner: Baby Kale And Cabbage Salad

Day 18

Breakfast: Mozzarella & Olive Cakes
Lunch: Roasted Cod With Cabbage
Dinner: Roasted Caramelized Root Vegetables

Day 19

Breakfast: Veg Mix And Blackeye Pea Burritos
Lunch: Baked Haddock With Rosemary Gremolata
Dinner: Chili Vegetable Skillet

Day 20

Breakfast: Fluffy Almond Flour Pancakes With Strawberries
Lunch: Asian-inspired Tuna Lettuce Wraps
Dinner: Spicy Potato Wedges

Day 21

Breakfast: Vegetable Polenta With Fried Eggs
Lunch: Herby Mackerel Fillets In Red Sauce
Dinner: Mushroom & Cauliflower Roast

Day 22

Breakfast: Spicy Black Bean And Poblano Dippers
Lunch: Baked Fish With Pistachio Crust
Dinner: Mini Crustless Spinach Quiches

Day 23

Breakfast: Berry-yogurt Smoothie
Lunch: Pan-fried Chili Sea Scallops
Dinner: Sardine & Caper Tagliatelle

Day 24

Breakfast: Honey Breakfast Smoothie
Lunch: Rosemary Wine Poached Haddock
Dinner: Rich Cauliflower Alfredo

Day 25

Breakfast: Granola & Berry Parfait
Lunch: Potato Lamb And Olive Stew
Dinner: Rigatoni With Peppers & Mozzarella

Day 26

Breakfast: Baked Honey Acorn Squash
Lunch: Chicken Drumsticks With Peach Glaze
Dinner: Caprese Pasta With Roasted Asparagus

Day 27

Breakfast: Tasty Lentil Burgers
Lunch: Deluxe Chicken With Yogurt Sauce
Dinner: Mozzarella & Asparagus Pasta

Day 28

Breakfast: Basic Brown Rice Pilaf With Capers
Lunch: Pork Chops In Tomato Olive Sauce
Dinner: Chickpea Salad With Tomatoes And Basil

INDEX

Cherry & Pine Nut Couscous 72
Chicken & Barley Soup 66
Chicken & Vegetable Skewers 36
Chicken Drumsticks With Peach Glaze 33
Chicken Sausage & Zucchini Soup 35
Chicken Souvlaki 38
Chicken With Bell Peppers 39
Chicken With Halloumi Cheese 37
Chickpea Salad With Tomatoes And Basil 54
Chili Vegetable Skillet 50
Cilantro-tomato Soup 69
Citrusy & Minty Farro 55
Cocktail Meatballs In Almond Sauce 36
Coconut Blueberries With Brown Rice 81
Cointreau Poached Pears 83
Collard Green & Rice Salad 67
Couscous & Cucumber Bowl 19
Creamy Tomato Hummus Soup 68
Cucumber Noodles With Goat Cheese 76

D

Deluxe Chicken With Yogurt Sauce 34
Dill Baked Sea Bass 27
Dill Smoked Salmon & Eggplant Rolls 25
Dulse, Avocado, And Tomato Pitas 15

E

Easy Grilled Pork Chops 41
Easy Walnut And Ricotta Spaghetti 61
Energy Granola Bites 79

F

Falafel Balls With Tahini Sauce 16
Fava And Garbanzo Bean Ful 58
Fluffy Almond Flour Pancakes With Strawberries 20
Fresh Mozzarella & Salmon Frittata 12

G

Garbanzo Patties With Cilantro-yogurt Sauce 81
Garlicky Zucchini Cubes With Mint 47
Granola & Berry Parfait 22
Greek Roasted Lamb Leg With Potatoes 40
Greek-style Chicken & Egg Bake 41
Green Bean & Rice Chicken Soup 69
Green Beans With Tahini-lemon Sauce 72
Grilled Eggplant "steaks" With Sauce 45
Grilled Za´atar Zucchini Rounds 43

O

Old-fashioned Pasta Primavera 55
Olive Mezze Platter 78
One-pot Linguine With Brussels Sprouts 60
Open-faced Margherita Sandwiches 13
Orange Mug Cakes 77

P

Pan-fried Chili Sea Scallops 32
Pan-fried Tuna With Vegetables 25
Panko Grilled Chicken Patties 35
Paprika Chicken With Caper Dressing 37
Parchment Orange & Dill Salmon 27
Parsley & Olive Zucchini Bake 46
Parsley Tomato Tilapia 25
Peppery Chicken Bake 37
Pork Chops In Tomato Olive Sauce 34
Pork Chops In Wine Sauce 40
Portuguese-style Chicken Breasts 40
Potato Lamb And Olive Stew 33
Prawns With Mushrooms 24
Pumpkin Soup With Crispy Sage Leaves 73

R

Raspberry & Nut Quinoa 56
Rice Pudding With Roasted Orange 82
Rich Beef Meal 39
Rich Cauliflower Alfredo 52
Rigatoni With Peppers & Mozzarella 53
Roasted Caramelized Root Vegetables 50
Roasted Carrot Ribbons With Mayo Sauce 76
Roasted Cod With Cabbage 29
Roasted Vegetables And Chickpeas 48
Roasted Veggies And Brown Rice Bowl 42
Rosemary Pork Loin With Green Onions 36
Rosemary Wine Poached Haddock 32

S

Salmon And Mushroom Hash With Pesto 26
Salt And Pepper Calamari And Scallops 24
Samosas In Potatoes 17
Sardine & Caper Tagliatelle 52
Sautéed Cabbage With Parsley 43
Seafood Cakes With Radicchio Salad 30
Shrimp & Salmon In Tomato Sauce 28
Shrimp And Pea Paella 29
Simple Lentil Risotto 57
Simple Spiced Sweet Pecans 84

Spanish-style Linguine With Tapenade 61
Speedy Granita 78
Spiced Hot Chocolate 82
Spiced Nut Mix 75
Spicy Black Bean And Poblano Dippers 21
Spicy Chicken Lentils 58
Spicy Haddock Stew 23
Spicy Potato Wedges 50
Spring Salad With Mustard Dressing 69
Sweet Chicken Stew 35
Sweet Potato Chickpea Buddha Bowl 44

T

Tasty Lentil Burgers 47
Tomato & Apple Salad With Walnuts 64
Tomato Eggs With Fried Potatoes 18
Turkey Pesto Pizza 74
Turkish Baklava 75
Turkish Eggplant And Tomatoes Pide With Mint 18

V

Veg Mix And Blackeye Pea Burritos 20
Vegan Lentil Bolognese 42
Vegetable Polenta With Fried Eggs 21
Vegetarian Mediterranean Stew 71
Vegetarian Patties 78
Veggie-stuffed Portabello Mushrooms 45

W

Whipped Feta Spread 66
White Pizzas With Arugula And Spinach 14
Wild Rice With Cheese & Mushrooms 59
Wilted Dandelion Greens With Sweet Onion 47

Printed in Great Britain
by Amazon

26509633R00051